HAVANA DECO

HAVANA DECO

ALEJANDRO G. ALONSO

PEDRO CONTRERAS

MARTINO FAGIUOLI

W. W. NORTON & COMPANY

NEW YORK · LONDON

First published by CV Export S.a.s. Divisione Libri Bologna Italy. Published in Spanish and Italian under the title LA HABANA DECO and published in English.

Copyright © 2007, 2003 by CV Export S.a.s., Divisione libri
First American Edition 2007

For information about permission to reproduce selections from this book, write to Permissions, W.W. Norton & Company Inc., 500 Fifth Avenue, New York, NY 10110

Manufacturing by KHL Printing
Book design by Jonathan D. Lippincott
Production manager: Leeann Graham

Library of Congress Cataloging-in-Publication Data
Alonso, Alejandro G.
   [La Habana deco. English]
   Havana deco / Alejandro G. Alonso, Pedro Contreras, Martino Fagiuoli.
— 1st American ed.
      p. cm.
   Published in Spanish under the title La Habana deco.
   Includes bibliographical references and index.
   ISBN 978-0-393-73232-0 (hardcover)
1. Art deco—Cuba—Havana. 2. Art, Cuban—Cuba—Havana—20th century.
1. Contreras, Pedro, 1943– II. Fagiuoli, Martino, 1956– III. Title.
   N6603.5.A78A4613 2007
   709.7291'09041—dc22

                                                          2007007046

ISBN 13: 978-0-393-73232-0

W.W. Norton & Company, Inc., 500 Fifth Avenue, New York, NY 10110
www.wwnorton.com

W.W. Norton & Company Ltd., Castle House, 75/76 Wells Street, London W1T 3QT

0 9 8 7 6 5 4 3 2 1

CONTENTS

PREFACE

There are parts of Havana that make you think it is one of the most beautiful cities in the world. At the same time, it is a city of contradictions. If you take a leisurely walk at night along the Malecón, the seawall hugging the coast, you will pass through the elegance of Habana Vieja (Old Havana) to the greatly deteriorated Centro Habana and onto El Vedado, with its large shade trees and remains of what once were sprawling one-family houses. As you continue along the water, you will see ordinary Cubans—lovers, friends, hustlers, rappers—sitting on the wall, alone or holding hands, staring out to sea or watching pedobikes, barely restored '40s American cars, rickety Russian Ladas, and brand new Mercedes cruising along the accompanying roadway. You will suddenly be hit by a whiff of kerosene or a spray of seawater as a wave dashes into the rocks. You will most definitely hear a Cuban *bolero* or *son* escaping from a nearby apartment. A gigantic moon will rise out of the ocean.

Havana is a sensuous city, pulsing, alive.

Havana Deco is a paean to Havana's gorgeous architectural gems of the '20s, '30s, and '40s, the heyday of the world Art Deco rage. Each city puts its own stamp on a movement—Paris's Art Nouveau became Germany's Jugendstil and Vienna's Sezession style: Deco is sultrier in Havana, jazzed up, with Afro-Cuban elements especially in its photography, painting, and graphic arts. Many of the decorative motifs—fruits, birds, arabesques—are Latinized, and Deco structures are often flanked by a variety of palms, dracaenas, and banana trees. Though most of the marble was imported, doorways, furniture, and interiors make frequent use of cedar and mahogany, Cuba's precious native trees. Where elsewhere you see corridors and courtyards, in Cuba there are airy porches galore.

Two outstanding Art Deco structures—one purist, the other eclectic—are the Edificio Emilio Bacardí and the Hotel Nacional, both finished in 1930. The former, with a bronze bat poised on its ziggurat crown, stands stylishly on the cusp between Habana Vieja and Centro Habana, while the Nacional—designed by McKim, Mead and White and visited by the likes of Buster Keaton, Marlene Dietrich, Winston Churchill, and Meyer Lansky—lords over its own imposing bluff, facing the sea.

In Havana, Deco homes pop up in suburban Vedado buttressed by utilitarian Soviet structures and appear nearly forgotten in poor outlying suburbs under a canopy of ficus trees. And some of the most stunning examples of Deco are the crypts in the Colon Cemetery.

By including furniture, light fixtures, grill work, doorways, and tiles, Alejandro Alonso, Pedro Contreras, and Martino Faguioli have created a stunning view of how Deco took Havana by storm in the pre-Castro years. This book bears testimony to the need to protect and restore Havana's Deco past to the same degree that the guardians of Cuba's architectural history have restored and replenished dozens of buildings in Habana Vieja (named a UNESCO World Heritage Site in 1982). Until the day when everyone can see these gems firsthand, we are grateful to the authors for this lovingly photographed and written book.

David Unger

INTRODUCTION

After emerging in Paris, Art Deco quickly traveled to the United States, where it would form deep roots and from where, in just a few years, it would spread throughout practically the entire world. From the outset one must clarify that the designation Art Deco is recent, deriving from a reevaluation of the style that took place in 1966. In its own time it was known as Moderno, Arte Moderno or Arte Nuevo (Modern, Modern Art or New Art), and it referred to expressions of an eminently decorative character. These were defined during an era framed by the two twentieth-century world wars as simultaneously classical, symmetrical and rectilinear, and glamorous.

Art Deco's gestation as a movement occurred between 1908 and 1912, reaching the pinnacle of its development between 1925 and 1935. Its influence lasted longer, in some areas until the beginning of the 1950s. The year 1925 is especially important. It was the year of the Paris Exposition Internationale des Arts Décoratifs et Industrieles Modernes, from which Art Deco's principal stylistic form became known and distributed worldwide. The contemporary name derives from the very title of the exhibit—Arts Décoratifs—hence Art Deco. The style is the cumulative result of such varied influences as Art Nouveau, Cubism, Fauvism, the Bauhaus, and Italian Futurism, combined with an interest in primitive and ancient art from the Orient, Egypt, Africa and the Americas. It has been pointed out that Art Deco emerged as a light, graceful innovation stimulated by the Ballets Russes during their performances in the French capital. It quickly became evident, however, that the style was changing into a simple, austere expression of modern life in the Machine Age, which nonetheless main-

Caricature of the Grupo de Minoristas (February 1927) by Massaguer.

The Flapper, drawing by Massaguer. *Social*, March 1926.

The legendary Catalina Lasa in all her glory.

Tropical interpretation of Deco style. Sketch by D. Alsina. *Arquitectura y Decoración*, September 1931.

tained a sophisticated and elegant—let us say, chic—look. Thus, the difference between Art Deco and its roots lies in the intensity of the function of its stylistic principles, its decorative nature—as applied arts—and, of course, the originality of its own contributions.

Art Deco penetrated contemporary life so deeply that it soon influenced people's clothing and their behavior, their means of travel and work, and the way they spent their free time, spearheaded by American movies and entertainment magazines. Art Deco molded leisure and the modern culture. Its reach was most marked in tangible things: movie theaters, apartment and office buildings, skyscrapers, interior decoration, lighting, sculpture, painting, graphic design (posters, notices, illustrations, typography), fashion, public works and structures of all kinds. In recalling such representative New York towers as the Chrysler Building or the Empire State Building, one can clearly imagine Art Deco in its entirety. There are many clear examples of the first stage of Art Deco, known as Zigzag Modern, that would later evolve into Classic Modern and Streamline, in addition to regional modalities. These provide a schematic order that notes distinct Deco stages which in fact often appeared concurrently or alternately in time.

This volume, conceived primarily as a photographic tour through the Cuban capital, captures images through the lens of the Italian photographer Martino Fagiuoli; this edition includes additional photos by Alejandro Alonso. The book is a reflection on the presence of Art Deco in Havana: its arrival and impact, the structures still remaining in the city, and on how different expressions in architecture and other visual arts—graphic arts, painting, and sculpture—assumed the characteristics of the style. Although it was not limited to the capital—rather, it encompassed the entire nation—Art Deco was most highly concentrated in Havana.

Art Deco developed on Caribbean soil within a particular framework. Its initial boundary lay within the first government of General Gerardo Machado (a man later to become a bloody tyrant), who was determined to retain his power through reelection. Its later boundary fell within the last mandate of another military figure—Fulgencio Batista—who returned to power through a coup in 1952. Between these two milestones Cubans endured the assumption of power by one or the other, fraudulent elections, and the indifference of high-level politicians to the needs of the nation. During this time there were two economic crises, a world war, a national revolution in 1933, with its resulting frustrating sequel, the second Constitution of the Republic, an American intervention and the omnipresent influence of American culture in all aspects of national life.

Conceptually speaking, the always cosmopolitan, open attitude of Cuba's people—a mixture of all races from which surges its major dynamic force—is fundamental. Other contributing elements are Cuba's natural beauty and climate, as well as its privileged geographical position, all of which have made the island simultaneously vulnerable and appealing. Finally, a last distinguishing factor: its immense and renowned ability to assimilate.

The first signs of Art Deco appeared during a time of consistent nationalist affirmation. All cultural circles experienced this impact. Its most conspicuous representative was Nicolás Guillén, a mixed-race poet who was able to translate the rhythm of the popular Cuban music called "son" (from which Latin "salsa" is derived) to its universal form of poetic verse.

The legitimate goal of this powerful movement, which included literature, music and the visual arts, was to be internationally understood while it simultaneously maintained authenticity. One example of the zeal to effect this goal was without doubt the birth of the Grupo de Minoristas, a social activist move-

The artist Enrique García Cabrera (at left) and two unidentified companions, ca. 1935.

Decorative drawings by Karreño. *Social,* April 1930.

The original plan for the underground Havana Bay Tunnel was initially a Deco project (1949).

On two facing pages: French posters and advertisement for the furniture store La Moda. *Social*, November 1930.

ment not aligned with any political party. Rather, the Grupo was created and supported by the most prominent intellectuals at all levels. Its role in the launching of these first efforts was of crucial importance. The magazine *Social*—and the large Grupo de Minoristas who were its friends, and, more importantly, its contributors—holds a distinguished place in any analysis of the role of publications in the spread of the new modes of expression. These contributors collaborated in the task of elevating a bourgeoisie intent on demonstrating its business prowess.

A case in point is that of Alejo Carpentier, one of the most highly regarded twentieth-century Spanish-language novelists. Carpentier, also a musicologist and essayist, sent writings from Paris that covered nearly all areas of culture, from the music of Stravinsky to the paintings of Picasso. To this he added critical comments on Parisian fashions (accepted as an artistic discipline), which he authored under the pseudonym Jacqueline. All this was transmitted through the pages of *Social*, founded and headed by a Minorista, Conrado Walter Massaguer.

Fundamental aspects of this period, whether automation, feminism or the definition of a national identity achieved by way of its racial roots, were seen through the somewhat mundane lens of this periodical. Nonetheless, these issues appeared alongside depictions of a costume ball with a historical theme or the wedding of a tycoon's daughter. Within its pages also appeared the splendid home built by Catalina Lasa, who would become a legend for reasons other than her patronage of the most highly noted Deco interiors at the early date—for Cuba—of 1927.

This year was crucial for Cuban art. It saw not only the building of the first structures in this style, but also the early visual artworks by modernist national artists, efforts that were indisputably preceded by those of the graphic artists

The artists Mario Carreño, Enrique Riverón and Antonio Gattorno with their oil paintings. New York City, ca. 1940.

published in art and entertainment magazines. In order to better understand these works, it must be noted that some of the great examples of Art Deco architecture that remain are associated with diverse sources. There are those generated by private initiatives at the dawn of Cuba's unique artistic presence. Immediately afterward, as early as 1930, two of the best hospital complexes found in Cuba would be designed by Govantes and Cabarrocas, thanks to the support of Gerardo Machado, a leader who was otherwise disastrous for Cuba. These, as well as the construction of the grand Carretera Central (Central Highway), correspond to the period of his first constitutional presidency. One cannot deny the relationship between the Monumental Modern and various backyard dictators in both Latin America and fascist Europe, a relationship which in Cuba gave rise to the hospitals, plazas, asylums, barracks and civic institutions built under the mandate of that unique authoritarian figure Fulgencio Batista. This is not a chance occurrence, since this Art Deco style, colossal in its sensibility, is strongly linked to the psychology of such personalities. All this is part of the overall picture; what remains are the magnificent buildings that still echo that particular period.

These examples are sometimes grand, sometimes small and intimate. Many important happenings, momentous historic events and magnificent works of art propelled an era so significant for Cuba that, like a resplendent gem, it conveys the legacy of Art Deco in a national voice.

Bronze relief for an ornamental light source on Calle Marina by the sculptor Juan José Sicre, 1931.

Convention and Sports Center designed by the architect José Pérez Benitoa, completed in 1942 and demolished years later to make way for the extension of the Havana Malecón.

Interior of the Catherine Rudolf Fashion Salon, ca. 1940, according to the plan by the architect Emilio de Soto.

Drawing by Carlos Enríquez, one of the first-generation Cuban "modern" painters, made during his stay in New York, 1930.

ARCHITECTURE

THE ARCHITECTURE

Images of the most important pavilions of the 1925 Paris Exposition Internationale des Arts Décoratifs et Industrieles Modernes arrived in Cuba when *Social* magazine published an illustrated report featuring the exhibit in the October 1925 issue, just four months after the magazine's inauguration. The first echoes of the Art Deco movement were felt barely two years later, with what is acknowledged to be the first private residence designed entirely in this style, in 1927, by the architect José Antonio Mendigutía for Francisco Argüelles in the Miramar residential area. Coincidentally, in the not-so-elegant neighborhood of Cayo Hueso in Centro Habana, the architect Leonardo Morales had envisioned a five-story building, whose construction was completed in December of 1927. This changes the historiography of the style, since the Edificio Bacardí (1930) was thought to be the first tall Art Deco building constructed in Havana. Moreover, it is interesting that the style's initiation came about as a parallel between a private residential dwelling in western Havana and a tall building in Centro Habana. They were distinct from each other from the standpoint of constructive typology, but they were created in the same spirit. In addition to publications, travel to Europe by architects, professionals and wealthy families also contributed to seeding this idea among developers and among those who could finance these projects. This was how architect Rodríguez Castells changed his original idea for the Bacardí, and in the same manner, others created the marvelous "modern" interior for the mansion (1924–1927) designed in the Italian Renaissance style for Juan Pedro Baró and Catalina Lasa. This mansion was designed by the architects Govantes and Cabarrocas. Each one in its own way is a unique event in the Art Deco architecture of Havana: paradigmatic but impossible to imitate.

The architect J. M. Bens Arrate reflected on how the year 1928 marked the beginning of the reaction against the Spanish Renaissance style, which had arrived via Miami and California. The list of the best homes built in that year drafted by Arrate included both the Mendigutía and Catalina Lasa mansions and other residences built in the historicist style, thus bringing to light the conflict between past and present. Next he noted how, thanks to modern lifestyles, residential neighborhoods were becoming less congested and Havana was joining the ranks of the great world capitals. This period saw the expansion of the city toward the west and, later, in other directions through suburban zones. One can see that this new approach to architecture was tied to the intellectual development of a nation whose greatest resource lay in the possibilities for interchange afforded by its geographical location.

Art Deco did not burst upon a pure environment, since the same professionals who would continue to design within the usual historical styles simultaneously incorporated Deco forms. The output of two firms, Morales y Compañía and Govantes y Cabarrocas, are cases in point. Architectural practice was heavily inclined toward Deco stylistic elements, which left their mark in roofed areas, parks, and a great variety of structures. This was possible thanks to the labor of knowledgeable, well-informed architects who were also talented sculptors, and to the work of simple technicians who showed a great capacity for creative assimilation. Artists and artisans made important contributions toward unifying each architectural design element into the total Deco concept. Every unifying aspect—from the general composition of the façade and its parapets, to the gates, doors, windows, ornamental grilles and keyholes—would extend to the interior of private homes and public buildings. Art Deco was widespread and long-lived in the capital. Although one can find examples of the style in practically all areas of Havana, the following zones are of particular interest: the densely populated Centro Habana, where the works of renowned architects coexist with those of anonymous developers; El Vedado, where a tall building such as the Edificio López Serrano would occupy a singular place in the urban tapestry of one- and two-story homes; Miramar, with some good examples of middle-class houses, the beach social clubs and "modern" churches; and the combination of Plaza Finlay and the nearby hospitals of Marianao, which are large buildings designed in the Monumental Modern style. This Art Deco period began in the late 1920s and continued until the Streamline style appeared in the car dealerships in the Cayo Hueso neighborhood and in a late period building of the early 1950s, the Gran Templo Masónico.

EDIFICIO EMILIO BACARDÍ

One of the best examples of Havana's Art Deco style is the Edificio Emilio Bacardí, a project completed in 1930 that brought together Esteban Rodríguez Castells, architect Rafael Fernández Ruenes, and engineer José Menéndez. The building is located at the corner of Calles Monserrate and San Juan de Dios in Old Havana. At the time of its completion in 1930 it was the tallest structure in the central zone. It has daring elements: its stepped design rising atop the block base, a chromatic exterior, and the figure of a bat at the top of its tower. The building is twelve stories high. Originally, five floors were designated as office rental space and the remainder allotted to the company after which it was named. The decision concerning the project was the result of a rigorous contest won by the team that presented a Neo-Renaissance concept; this changed substantially with the designers' visit to Paris. In fact, all this began much earlier—in 1861—when the Catalan Don Facundo Bacardí, who lived in Santiago de Cuba, bought a humble distillery from the Englishman John Nunes. He dedicated himself to the pursuit of a new formula for removing all the impurities from crude rum without destroying its bouquet and characteristic flavor. If someone were to ask why a bat is the company emblem, the answer would lie in the ambiguous realm between fact and legend. It seems that one of the eaves of the manufacturing plant in Santiago housed a colony of the odd flying mammals. Don Facundo did not chase them out, since the bat represents union, loy-

The Edificio Bacardí was intended to be an especially daring design. This is clearly indicated given the building's mass and the use of lavish materials. There is speculation regarding the many issues that resulted in the acceptance of the radical changes made to the original plans. These revisions occurred when its principal architect experienced the full impact of the Exposition of Decorative Arts. No matter how new the style was, however, its heritage was apparent: in this case, the obvious antecedent was the supposed cradle of Western civilization. Thus, the choice of a Babylonian ziggurat as a point of reference and the strong beauty of the enameled terracotta used in the façade, which reminds us of the creators of the incredible Gate of Ishtar, is not a matter of chance. The prestige of history coupled with "modern" art; Babylon and Paris embrace.

Views and details of the Edificio Emilio Bacardí (1930); Esteban Rodríguez Castells, architect. The enameled terracotta is by Maxfield Parrish.

alty, confidence, and discretion both in his own country and in European heraldry. This Art Deco jewel in Cuba's capital is called the Edificio Emilio Bacardí in homage to the notable Cuban, born in Santiago de Cuba, who was the eldest son of Don Facundo. Don Emilio (1844–1922), who was an aficionado of poetry and painting from childhood, made important contributions to his country's independence. While mayor of his native city, he proposed the establishment of a museum, inaugurated in 1899, for the preservation of memorabilia from the wars of independence. This museum is named after him. He also created a library annexed to the museum, the Academia Municipal de Bellas Artes, and other public works.

The inscription that identifies the building appears on the façade and is inscribed into the red granite of the base.

HOTEL NACIONAL

Located on Havana's coastal cliffs, the Hotel Nacional de Cuba holds a privileged site, given its marvelous panoramic views. The project was made possible thanks to an agreement (signed by Gerardo Machado, then president of the Republic) by which the Cuban government gave land rights to the builder while retaining permanent use of the hotel's Presidential Suite for official functions. After sixty years of operation by its American builder, the hotel would become the property of the Cuban government without further monetary compensation. Work was completed in just two years, and the Hotel Nacional was inaugurated on the evening of December 30, 1930. The extraordinary architecture is characterized by an eclectic sense that results from a mixture of stylistic factors—including its exterior ornamentation—usually associated with Art Deco. Although this spot was the site of some very important historic events, the character and ambience of the Nacional are defined by the glamour of the movies and its stars. Buster Keaton and Johnny Weissmuller, Ava Gardner and Frank Sinatra, Fred Astaire and Rita Hayworth, Tyrone Power, Cesar Romero and Marlene Dietrich, María Félix and Jorge Negrete were all guests of the ho-

Hotel Nacional de Cuba (1930); McKim, Mead & White, designers, New York; Purdy & Henderson Company, builders. Until 1930, American influence was very strong. This included the direct work of American architects who disseminated styles ranging from regional variations with historicist traits to the so-called universal classical style. Contemporary construction and decoration were employed in the Hotel Nacional. Within its generally eclectic line, one finds traces of a Spanish past in the floor tiles and coffered ceilings of the lobby. Deco details include both carved and applied stone reliefs, which appear on balconies, balustrades, pinnacles, ornamental peaks and, in general, the exterior decorations, which fit together with the chic stylistic plane typical of Art Deco. This is further proof of the great expansion of the style in Cuba.

tel. Politicians such as Winston Churchill and the infamous Mafia dons Meyer Lansky and Lucky Luciano also stayed there. All sought the environment of this enclave characterized by leisure, glamour, and an optimism that resisted tropical hurricanes and economic crises and which arose as a bastion of the Deco lifestyle.

EDIFICIO LÓPEZ SERRANO

The Edificio López Serrano (1932) represents a high level of the elegant sobriety typical of the New York skyscrapers built after the economic crash. A magnificent example of this style is Rockefeller Center. The Serrano design shows a certain restraint in the application of resources, even more striking when one considers a classic skyscraper in comparison. The building, designed by Ricardo Mira and engineered by Miguel Rosich, has a ten-story base block. The tower above the base consists of four stepped stories of the type associated with Art Deco constructions. A promotional pamphlet of the period for what was then the most modern building in Latin America connotes an image of comfort, cleanliness and luxury. The new, massive edifice took its name from the real estate tycoon, a multimillionaire businessman whose father, José López Rodríguez, known as "Pote," achieved notoriety during the 1921 Crash when he committed suicide, believing himself to be ruined—although he had a bank account that contained 11 million pesos.

The building features steel construction and brick walls. The ornamentation, although simple, is primarily based on plant motifs and appears on entryways, doors, windows and friezes. The building's stylistic unity is supported by the excellent terrazzo of its walkways and the tiles found inside its apartments, all of which strictly adhere to design concepts. The vestibule is a magnificent extension of this grandeur, highlighted by its floor, which contains a radial design,

This and following pages: details, Edificio López Serrano (1932); Ricardo Mira, architect; Miguel Rosich, engineer.

the careful treatment afforded to its ceiling by its deliberate lighting, and by its Moroccan-red marble-veneered walls. The nickel silver panel designed by Enrique García Cabrera expresses the theme of progress and speed and is a fitting culmination to an integrated design concept. Rising out of an area of low-lying houses typical of those found in El Vedado, the Edificio López Serrano presents a considerably modern presence within its surroundings.

SUBURBAN AREAS

In the year 1900 there were a quarter of a million *habaneros*. Twenty-nine years later the number of Havana's inhabitants easily surpassed the half-million mark. The causes of this demographic explosion included the arrival of Spaniards who settled there, as well as a small number of Americans. El Vedado, which played a pioneer role in the development of the city toward the west, initially received a substantial infusion of Cubans struggling for independence; these were generally wealthy. Then an economically powerful—but less exclusive—group occupied the area, a population that found its wealth in the boom years precipitated by the rise in sugar prices during World War I. Grand, eclectic mansions alternated with small, modest houses. However, all construction was adjusted to conform to municipal building regulations as, for example, whether small or large gardens should be placed in front of the property, how lateral walkways would separate one dwelling from another, and the distance between house and sidewalk. This created a typology that in some ways regulated the structure of the middle-class home. Thus, the central atrium favored in Spanish homes was replaced by the equally functional central hallway, which opened to each bedroom. When the very rhythm of the Machine Age stimulated the arrival of the new style, private dwellings were ready to incorporate this stylistic vocabulary with ease. Around 1925, the city had already crossed the Almendares River. Mi-

The home of Manuel López Chávez (1932), by the architect Esteban Rodríguez Castells, is one of the first in the style and the best preserved of its kind. It has magnificent decorative designs in stucco, glass and metal. The unity of the whole distinguishes this structure. Along with other early Art Deco buildings in Havana, it develops the issue of private suburban housing, which carried the weight of tradition to architecture on the national level.

A home on Calle Porvenir, Lawton.

The two-story house as a prototype of the private home proliferated in suburban areas and extended to the capital. The structure made use of a logical layout, which placed social areas on the lower floor and the bedrooms (private areas) on the floor above. The word *repartos* was used to describe urban areas where traditional historicist buildings continued to be built and where there was, nonetheless, room for the numerous structures that expressed an obvious need for modernity. The assimilation of Art Deco (then called "Arte Nuevo" or "Moderno") took on distinguishing features according to the characteristics of particular areas: the more luxurious homes were built in the more affluent neighborhoods to the west of Havana; to the south were the modest homes where the petite bourgeoisie had settled.

ramar, an upper- and upper-middle-class neighborhood, was founded here, in addition to several other neighborhoods (*repartos*) named after landowners or sponsors (Kohly, Nicanor del Campo, etc.). Because of its deference to urban design criteria and the high quality of its structures, El Vedado became a model for the new suburban areas.

More modest suburbs were created to the south of the constantly growing city. Similarly, some of these were also named after their developers or landowners, such as Lawton and Santos Suárez. This area was populated by an influx of the national bourgeoisie, as well as workers, who built homes within a varied range of possibilities and renderings. Even here, the interest in the new is seen in the details executed by highly skilled artisans. In simple homes one can often find a small luxury such as an interesting piece of metalwork or a delicately designed carved wooden door in a clearly modern style. Art Deco's adaptive strengths accompanied these developments, demonstrating the style's capacity for integration within a given physical environment. The list of grand mansions is short (the interior of the Catalina Lasa home holds first place). However, there are some excellent examples of upper-middle-class homes (such as those of López Chávez, Argüelles, Tamargo, Dr. Clemente Inclán,

Left and below: the home of Salomón Kalmanowitz (1936), Calle 28, no. 4517, Alturas de Miramar; Ángel López Valladares, architect.

Right: homes in Miramar and Lawton, where the assimilation of Streamline is apparent (rounded angles, fretwork, narrow bands of tiles) and the occasional presence of the floral patterns of a previous era.

Below: a home on Calle 28, no. 4506 (1936), Kohly neighborhood; Ángel López Valladares, architect.

Home of Dr. Clemente Inclán (1930) in Miramar; Pedro Martínez Inclán, architect.

among others). However, one finds a real proliferation of homes in the "modern" style on another, often very modest level, which were added to this movement in the simplest way possible: by the use of a cast cement panel over a main entrance.

PORCHES

Eugenio Batista, one of the pioneers of contemporary Cuban architecture, distinguished university professor and creator, as well, of major works during the 1930s, '40s, and '50s, maintained that there were three traditional elements worthy of being retained as architectural constants: window blinds, courtyards, and porches. Those elements are all related to the island's climate, the Cuban

lifestyle, and the Cuban mystique. However, porches in particular serve to establish passageways, areas of light and shade; they are spaces intended to induce a sensation of pleasure in the occupants or those entering the buildings. The growing city adapted to a considerable degree the solution of doorways for one- and two-story middle-class dwellings intended to provide spaces for family use. It thus became an ideal area for recreation and relaxation, for friendly intercourse and enjoyment of the cool of the afternoon and early evening. Splendid examples are abundant in the dwellings of the neighborhoods spreading to the west and south of the original center of Havana, which successfully ornamented them with graceful columns and pilasters. The zigzag and galloons characteristic of Deco brought out very creative and imaginative interpretations in keeping with the standards of the new style of dwellings in the suburban sections of El Vedado, Kohly, Santos Suárez and Ayestarán, contributing thereby to the creation of pleasant transitional spaces. There, the iron or masonry railings, with frequently incorporated modules of moulded cement that sometimes displayed Moderno geometric designs, charmingly set off areas marked by roof-support beams or window boxes. Everything was aimed at making social gatherings or time spent by persons waiting at the entrance of a house as agreeable as possible, in tangible demonstration of what made it possible for a style, newly appearing at the time, able to blend in in such a way as to achieve a close link with tradition.

IRON

"To our humble understanding, an original and modern artistic work in iron has not yet been built in Cuba."
This statement was made by Enrique Luis Varela, the very clever "modern" architect. It was November of 1932.
The Edificio Emilio Bacardí was open to the public, and there was already a body of work in iron created by
Cubans. The avant-garde Varela wanted more: a way to highlight the material itself while avoiding references
to its traditional use. This was a difficult task in a country where several factors (including the centuries-old
use of iron gates that provided protection against intruders, as well as ventilation) gave rise to a highly skilled
group of ornamental iron artisans. During this time there were excellent workshops, such as those of Basora,
Narciso Merino and Ramón García (El Motor).

Varela did not question the level of workmanship of these companies, but rather the abilities of their
clients. Notwithstanding Varela's opinions, the Art Deco period produced abundant and magnificent examples

of ironwork. The volute—a typical motif in the past—benefited from the modern style through the incorporation of iron zigzag filigree and the use of sharp angles. Sometimes iron and glass were used together in the making of doors, fences, gates and window locks, as well as in such simple elements as balcony partitions. Private homes, as well as multiple-dwelling structures, small businesses and industry, and tourist enclaves took advantage of the ductility of this material. Iron was even used successfully both as protection and as an ornamental element in the luxurious mausoleums of the Cementerio Cristóbal Colón.

In the city of Havana, home to many types of crafted iron for years, the new was added to what already existed. Ironwork evolved simultaneously with the distinct modalities of style. As form was simplified, so style became less complex and more fluid. Both became harmonious, decorative and functional factors without losing their links to tradition.

GARDENS

Beyond offering the convenience of a green space for family use, provision was made by the City of Havana for overseeing and classifying suburban residential areas that extended to the borders of the historical center of the city at a time when constraints that stunted growth or simply inhibited tastes, styles, and habits were already in place. The central courtyard of dwellings and colonial public buildings were disappearing to make way for a different organization of internal space. And so, gardens and small lateral spaces lent independence to the houses built with the incentive of incorporating nature into the family's daily rounds and recreation. Meanwhile, parks of moderate size where children could play arose on government lands or on properties donated by generous landowners. Areas were set aside for gatherings, simple diversions, or paying homage to forebears of the wars of independence with the erection of statues or commemorative monuments.

Both gardens and parks accepted the input from those Art Deco architects or builders who had bought into the possibilities of design offered by the open-air spaces, based upon the formal unity the style dictated. Ornamental light sources and benches, window boxes and other decorative elements, floors, sculptures, flower beds and fountains were to be given attention by those who, for the purpose of achieving an integrated design, broadened the scope of their work into those areas and created harmonious environments in which the geometry of building emphasized the organic spontaneity of nature, though not infrequently submitted to a streamlining approach. Again, the workshops of the

artisans came to the aid of the builders, who, carving volumes in stone or moulded cement in the form of vases (with or without flowers), outdoor furniture and other elements, justified decoration.

CENTRO HABANA

When the densely populated neighborhoods of Old Havana began encroaching on the "notables" of the city, the displacement did not occur to the south, but rather to the west toward El Vedado. Centro Habana (which was called simply La Habana) continued to uphold its traditional building structure using "adjacent" walls lacking lateral walkways separating one from the other. The city expanded across the thoroughfares of Belascoaín, San Lázaro, Reina, Monte, and many other parallel minor streets as well as other intersecting streets, which continued to be named after a person (Marqués González) or a mood (Soledad). This gave rise to the *barrios*, a word that perhaps best characterizes this kind of urban neighborhood. These were christened with names that carried strong popular appeal: La Punta (The Point), Los Sitios (The Places), Cayo Hueso (Key West). These areas saw the proliferation of a fortune-making institution, the collective dwelling. This kind of housing could project the populous dignity afforded to apartment buildings, as well as provide the habitat accorded to the pauper and found in the Havana *solar* (tenement-house). In other words, it was a tenement where entire families shared one room and in which the bathroom was used communally by dozens of tenants. For better or worse, Havana became the locale par excellence where the wealthy made purchases or procured prostitutes at the "sinners' corner" (Galiano and San Rafael), where small retailers set up shop and major stores such as La Casa Grande, El Encanto, and Fin de Siglo were established. Some of these no longer exist or have changed considerably. But on La Calzada de la Reina the imposing Almacenes

Facing page: detail of the Casa Suárez (1934), 368 Aguila, at San Miguel.

Left: doorway of the Casa Suárez. Center: balcony of a dwelling in Centro Habana. Right: chamfer on a building at Obispo and Villegas.

Ultra, with its richly ornamented Art Deco façade, still stands. The area contained apartment buildings that housed ground-floor retail space and embraced the new style—through their use of the elaborately ornamented stepped structure typical of Deco—while simultaneously paying homage to the past. A case in point is the Edificio Colonial, where one finds the generous use of balconies,

Facing page: apartment building (1939), Galiano and Zanja, Centro Habana.

Left: apartment buildings on Calle San Lázaro.

Following pages: details of the Edificio Colonial (1930), Calle Reina, no. 315, between Campanario and Lealtad, Centro Habana; Francisco Villaciergo, architect.

Left to right: façade of the Edificio Colonial, detail of the Edificio Colonial, detail of a house on Calle Estrella and detail of a house on Calle Gervasio.

ironwork, French windows, and transom windows made of milky glass to filter the intense natural light. The building undoubtedly maintains its link to tradition without discarding "modern" traits. The *barrio* of Pueblo Nuevo has an especially high concentration of Art Deco structures: nearly half of the buildings in the area are in this style or, at the very least, contain some details related to it. These constructions are the result of anonymous builders and able artisans who left an invaluable testament in ironworks, decorative frieze panels and door and window carpentry. Here spaces are small and balconies large, giving this neighborhood a distinctive and unique character. The structures in Centro

Details of an apartment building on Calle
Estrella, corner of Calle Ángeles.

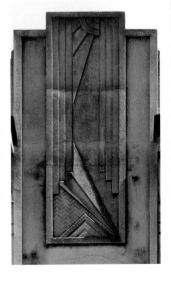

Habana are plentiful and interesting, but some, like
the building for the Casa Suárez, are outstanding.
Thus, Centro Habana is still enhanced by the many
sites that make the area a treasure trove of all
things Art Deco: the exquisite and the popular
combined.

The work of renowned architects and
anonymous builders left their mark on
Centro Habana. Frequently, finishing
touches gave exteriors a holistic unity.
These often included materials such as
sand silica, mica or marble dust. The
abundance of balconies with iron grille
work, as well as friezes and bas-relief
panels made of molded cement,
provided graceful Deco accents to
the area.

Facing page: apartment building (1936), Calles Ánimas and Gervasio.

Above: residence (1934–1937) Calle San Rafael, no. 1165; Emilio Azcué, architect.

Left: detail of an apartment building, Carlos III and San Francisco. Center: detail of an apartment building (1940) on Calle Marina. Right: detail of an apartment building (1938), San Nicolás and Neptuno.

DECORATIVE PANELS

If there is one factor through which the Art Deco presence in the city can be felt on a generalized level, it is the use of ornamental friezes. This includes not only the reliefs created by artists, but also the anonymous creations of cast cement found both in grand works as well as in small suburban homes, where they were used to give structures a modern flavor. These panels, as well as other elements, were made in area workshops, where the motifs were carved into wood prototypes. The originals were then cast in plaster and molded in cement (if they were to be placed outdoors) or in plaster (if they were destined for an indoor space). Some designs were imported directly from the United States; architects also submitted sketches, which were then interpreted in the workshops. Other designs were simply chosen from catalogues, while another group was the result of inspired expert artisans working directly at the building sites.

If a frieze or border was required, an order was drawn up in meters or *varas* according to the Spanish

system. This method of propagating the new style subsequently caused it to assume the characteristics of mass production, in tune with the Machine Age. This is not to say that this method was created for Art Deco. Previously, great estates and public buildings constructed in the Eclectic and Art Nouveau styles had already used this method in order to provide those structures with an "artistic" touch. One cannot deny the furor that developed during the Deco period. The astounding variety of scale used to manufacture these elements leads to the conclusion that they were in great favor and even greater demand. For once, the most sophisticated architects as well as the modest developers were in agreement concerning the use of design elements that would stamp their works with the distinctive seal of craftsmanship. As for the motifs, those that were not geometric heavily favored flowers, fruits—the tropics as represented by the pineapple—and occasionally, animals. In short, the repertoire was stylistically diverse, technically well executed and economically viable.

Very plain in design, the building on Belascoaín (now Padre Varela) and San José has the distinction of being the first tall building (going back to 1927) designed in the style mentioned, in order to assume the priority thereby that had been given the Bacardi Building (1930), a point definitively established by the architect María Victoria Zardoya's research. Space is given over to porches on the ground floor, an element that is added to the series of roofed areas for pedestrian traffic provided for by official regulation on important streets such as the one it faces. The designer was Leonardo Morales, an open-minded architect who assimilated historical styles as part of his interpretation of Art Deco.

Alejandro Capó Boada was the architect of the 1938 tall building located at Monserrate and San Juan de Dios, precisely at the edge of Centro Habana's historic center. It is the neighborhood, separated only by Calle San Juan de Dios, of the illustrious Bacardi Building, which was built earlier. Its location could very well explain the lack of porches, as is the case in most of the buildings of so-called Old Havana, the oldest sector of the city, whose building code accepted buildings flush with the sidewalk. We came upon a curious aspect of this project in the plans submitted with the application for the building permit: first, its eclectic style and, later, the request to increase beyond the allowable height by three stories, which also changed its formal adherence to Art Deco.

URBAN ATMOSPHERE

Observance of town-planning regulations motivated the features of a small two-story building on a very small plot of land. Since it was surrounded by heavily transited streets and a lack of available space, room had to be left for a porch, mandatory on Calle Infanta, where the main façade stood. The prevailing taste of the day—anti-conventional, mass-appeal—introduced unfamiliar

colorfulness and sharp contrasts, unusual in that period of construction, in two buildings on Hamel Alley. This locale is now recognized as the site of more or less spontaneous popular manifestations of the rite of *santería*, a project of a community character. A surprising element is how at the near skyline the Edificio Solimar, which belongs to the variant of Streamline Deco, insinuated itself into this area. Not far from there, a relatively small building within the Art Deco genre—at the corner of Calle Spada and 25th, hints at its stylistic link with two neighboring dwellings in a neighborhood like Cayo Hueso where, literally, everything is to be found. Also in Cayo Hueso, on Calle Marina, by the sea, there are three adjacent buildings that each display a different intensity in the handling of the Deco vocabulary. One is more or less faithful to the style, another shows proto-Moderno features, and the third incorporates decorative marine elements. The mixture, the alternation of languages, the surprising incursion that has no patience for an untainted district, unquestionably enhances the rich ambience of this attractive area.

"SKYSCRAPERS"

The "skyscrapers" of Havana assumed the Art Deco style as a result of an esthetic that was rapidly becoming dominant. Two of these buildings were erected in El Vedado for office use. One of them was created *ex novo* by the architect Rafael de Cárdenas, on Calle 23 between O and P. The building presents a vertical impulse: uninterrupted pilasters alternate with narrow stretches of walls with many windows. The second, on Calles G and I, resulted in the addition of three stories and a tower to an existing building after several renovations were carried out between 1947 and 1953 by the architect Ramón Bustos. The third is the Edificio Rodríguez Vázquez (1941), situated on Calle Galiano at Calle Concordia and built by the architects Fernando Martínez Campos and Pascual de Rojas. This Art Deco jewel has a similar configuration and projects an incomparable creative energy.

Facing page: building (ca. 1940), Calle Primera and Avenida de los Presidentes, El Vedado.

This page, top: entrance to the apartment tower of the Edificio Rodríguez Vázquez (1941), Calle Galiano between Concordia and Neptuno; Fernández Martínez Campos and Pascual Rojas, architects. Bottom: detail of the Ministerio del Trabajo, Calle 23 between O and P; El Vedado, Rafael de Cárdenas, architect.

Left: façade of the Edificio Rodríguez Vázquez.

OTHER BUILDINGS

Art Deco's proven flexibility allowed for its adaptation to a variety of exigencies. Following is a group of structures whose common features are their individual distinctiveness and the fact that these buildings were not designed for housing. A building located in the Calzada de la Reina, designed by the architects Cristóbal Díaz and Rafael de Cárdenas for the newspaper *El País*, is in the vanguard of the style. Glass covers a large portion of the façade, giving it the aspect of a real work environment and inspiring curiosity about the nature of the firms within its walls. Metal was used in the capitals of its ground-floor columns and in the band that crosses its entire front, giving it an image associated with industry. Similarly, but with the added interest invoked by sculpted work, a grand frieze runs horizontally across the entire façade.

In this cast cement frieze the Spanish artist Cándido Álvarez developed the theme of labor, intrinsic to the lexicon of the new, futuristic style. The simple

In 1926, Cervantes and Cultural S.A. merged. These were very prestigious firms: the first, Cervantes, founded in 1910 by Ricardo Veloso Guerra in the Reparto Galiano near Neptuno, was the first company in Havana to sell books on credit and had the largest inventory in the city; and the second was on Obispo and Bernaza, founded in 1890 by José López Rodríguez. After the successful merger they built other branches in Cuba and abroad as well as new headquarters, which proved central to literary and cultural circles.

Top: detail of the frieze of the building housing the newspaper *El País*, Calle Reina, no. 158, Centro Habana; Cristóbal Díaz and Rafael de Cárdenas, architects.

Above, left to right: façade of the *El País* building; details of the bookstore La Moderna Poesía (ca. 1941), Calle Obispo, corner Bernaza, Old Havana; Ricardo Mira, architect, and Miguel Rosich, engineer.

clock in its center is a reminder of the importance and value of time. The architectural style and ornamentation are perfectly adapted to function. The building for the Canada Dry Bottling Company (1946) on Calles Infanta and Amenidad in El Cerro, designed by Walter M. Cory, conveys a similar message through a completely different design. Here the distinguishing stylistic factor in its façade is the use of glass brick. Not very far from the *El País* building, but in another neighborhood—Old Havana—the bookstore La Moderna Poesía once again emphasizes how the Art Deco style supported several objectives: to be functional; to express the power of its sponsors; and to maintain the mutually beneficial relationship between architect and owner. José A. López Serrano was the patron of the tall building named after him and located in El Vedado. It was designed by Mira and Rosich, whose concept tends toward verticality. The developer again demanded the services of these architects in building La Moderna

Above and top: tobacco warehouse (1929), Calle Zanja, no. 310, Centro Habana; Emilio de Soto, architect.

Facing page: La Casa Quintana (1937), Calle Galiano, no. 304, between San Rafael and San Miguel, Centro Habana; Alejandro Capó Boada, architect.

Poesía, but the approach is completely different, given that the solid appearance of the structure and the efficient use of architectural masses suggest horizontality. The design is completely devoid of surface ornamentation since it rests absolutely on the aforementioned attributes. The metal letters of the signage are the only ornamental accent in the entire façade, which faces the busy intersection of Obispo and Bernaza. The exterior gives no hint of the spacious layout—almost an open area—which provides exhibit areas for book publishers. The building's blueprints were published in *Cuba: Arquitectura y Artes Similares* in 1941. A tobacco warehouse brings to mind Assyrian motifs through the well-proportioned ornamentation of its façade. The Estadio Universitario stands as an austere presence devoid of all adornment and the Casa Quintana as a graciously appointed structure. The long, narrow panels filled with plant motifs and the remarkable identifying sign found on the pharmacy on Calle 23 attracts many admirers. All of these structures convey diverse and interesting options while serving entirely distinct purposes.

Facing page: Estadio
Universitario (1940),
Calle Ronda.

Left and above: pharmacy on
Calle 23, El Vedado.

DOORWAYS

To accent an entrance, to define, from a formal and stylistic standpoint, the space that provides access to a structure, is as old as architecture itself, ever since it was transformed into a significant presence within the purview of artistic creation. Without reaching beyond Cuba's geographical framework and Cuban tradition itself, it should be noted that the attention given doorways came at a time during the colonial period when a taxonomy of all its component elements was being created. It is impossible to ignore the wooden leaves for blocking off and, at the same time, facilitating the swinging on hinges to permit passage. Its appearance was accompanied by an approach that extended to doorjambs and *modenaturas* (ornamental elements in the upper part of the door), so vigorously developed that it might well be dubbed the "Havana doorjamb" as a characteristic element in the entryway of eighteenth-century dwellings, churches and public buildings. Accordingly, a style like Deco was hard put to neglect the possibility of influencing those aspects particularly when the well-known expertise of the nation's craftsmen (carpenters, plasterers, ironworkers) who worked independently, as mem-

bers of cooperative workshops or as part of actual companies, were putting their services at the disposal of those who had overall responsibility for a project—that is, professional architects or ordinary builders.

The raw material for the doors was the high-quality lumber cut in forests where uncontrolled logging was permitted. This facilitated the widespread use of precious types—such as cedar, *ácana*, *sabicú*—according to the choice and taste of the investor. Plain boards, surfaces with various inlays in keeping with the dictates of style, simple geometrical patterns—all introduced varieties of nuance. Examining that zone, Centro Habana, with a high concentration of Deco buildings, can provide an ample catalogue of the ways entrances benefited from the treatment of elements—inherently utilitarian—aimed at guaranteeing personal security. Accordingly, the attention paid such factors was not confined to the doorjamb and the doors themselves, since their design was dominated by the doorjambs and the marquee (occasionally monumental or transformed into a mere accent) upon the lintels, where it also occurs in abbreviated relief, in the highly ornamental plaque and elongated vertical panel. All these factors pointed up the interest in making something somewhat individualized out of the entrance, an area that lent itself to the attractive presence of echoes of the style that welcomes the visitor and sees him out.

CINEMAS

Previous pages: Teatro Lutgardita (1932),
Calzada de Bejucal, no. 30901, Rancho
Boyeros; Evelio Govantes and Félix
Cabarrocas, architects.

Above and opposite: Detail and façade
of the Cine Arenal (1945), Avenida 41
and Calle 30, Reparto La Sierra.

Although movies arrived in Cuba before Art Deco, almost all the theaters built specifically for film were designed in this style. The Art Deco style was reflected in the interiors of the cinemas, which had specific technical requirements. It extended to the exteriors, where the style was expressed in different ways and at various levels of intensity. These standards were well integrated in the Cine Moderno (1930), designed by the architect Ernesto López Rovirosa, and found in Calzada de Jesús del Monte, which was then a lower-middle- and working-class suburb. Subsequent changes and poor preservation have damaged its appearance. The Teatro Lutgardita (1932), designed by Govantes and Cabarrocas, is radically different because of the contrast between the façade, with its spare use of Deco elements, and its interior, an outstanding example of an environment inspired by Mayan motifs. These regional alterations to the Art Deco style,

which resulted in a marked theatrical sense and in the development of a wide range of technical innovations, were unforeseen in this suburb of modest, Neocolonial homes. Saturnino Parajón designed a distinctive building, the Teatro Fausto (1938), on Paseo del Prado y Colón. Situated in an area of well-built eclectic homes, its purely modernistic façade makes an elegant break from its neighbors; this in spite of an open porch, mandated by local ordinance for pedestrian traffic. The technical advances and amenities incorporated into the building created great interest. For example, it was the first theater in Havana to boast of air conditioning. Its walls contained an internal interstice which effectively protected the theater from outside noise, and its front entrance used neon lights hidden behind metallic tubes (still in evidence today) to produce chromatic effects. These advances duly merited a façade that expressed its function with a modern vocabulary. The Teatro Arenal (1945) in Marianao exemplifies the aforementioned idea of creating theaters with a strong Art Deco identity through its somewhat exaggerated monumental scale.

In other Havana neighborhoods, more examples of this style were constructed, albeit on a smaller scale. Among these are the Infanta, Cuatro Caminos Rex Cinema-Duplex, and Manzanares theaters, none of which still stand. Among the very deteriorated are the Reina and the Verdún. The Cine-Teatro América (1941), at Galiano and Concordia, is also an excellent example. It was built as part of an architectural complex that included a preexisting theater, ground-floor businesses and a rental-apartment tower.

Teatro Fausto (1938), Paseo del Prado, no. 201, corner of Colón, Old Havana; Saturnino Parajón, architect.

Facing page: large decorative panel, Cine City Hall (1953), Avenida de Ayestarán, no. 473.

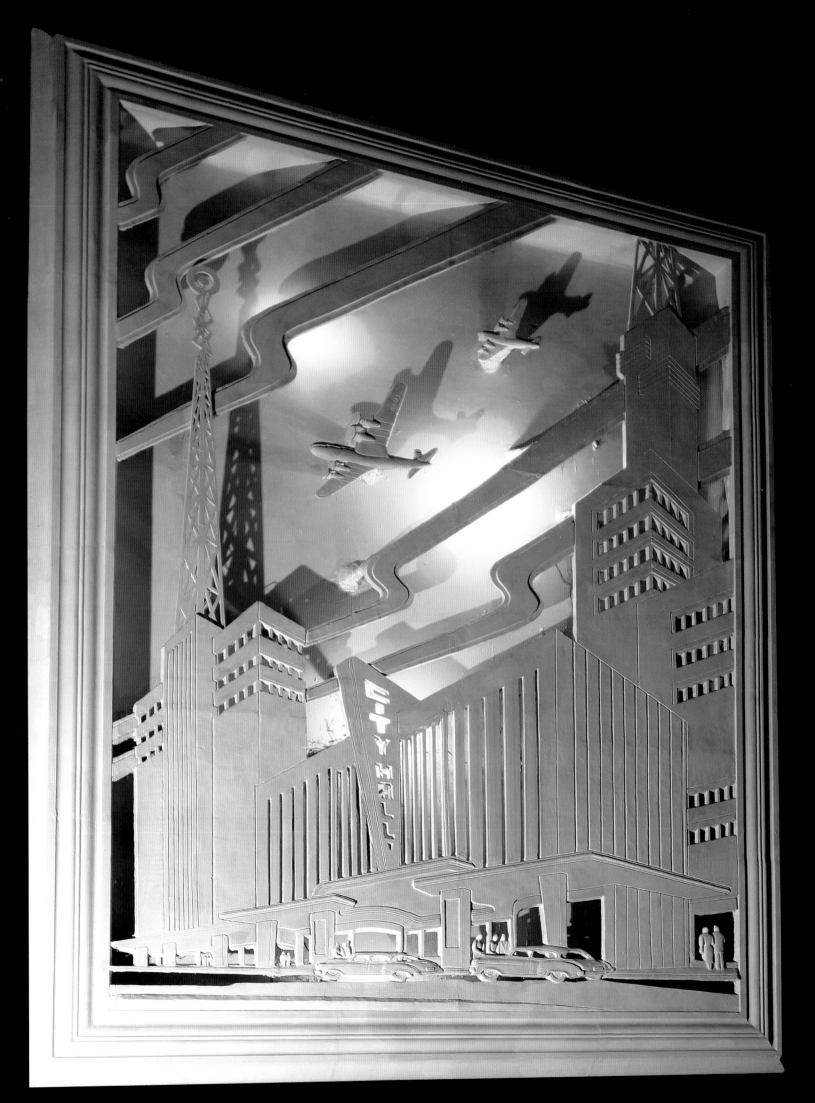

Deco design entered El Vedado by way of the private home. The "modern" home adopted the use of the hall in place of the central courtyard used previously. However, its ornamentation used typical Art Deco motifs and stepped design elements. Apartment buildings, influenced by the Edificio López Serrano, introduced a spatial distribution that allowed for convenient retail space on the lower floor and comfortable multiple living spaces on the upper floors. These areas benefited from a design that provided good lighting and ventilation. Among the most original is the Edificio Triángulo, located on Calles 23 and 20, El Vedado, by the architect Cristóbal Díaz, whose design made the building appear pleated. Private services and commercial businesses were located on the ground floor: a supermarket, a hardware store and a barbershop. The latter is still operating and retains some of its original Deco furnishings.

EL VEDADO

An area to the southwest of the city that runs parallel to the sea would play a major role in Havana's expansion. That section is El Vedado, built up during the last quarter of the nineteenth century. El Vedado takes its name from the land where construction was prohibited and where travel was restricted during the period when Cuba was a Spanish colony, a time when the area's strategic location was crucial to the city's defense. Its western border was the Almendares River, whereas the eastern border was Centro Habana and the wide Calle Infanta. The introduction of the "new," or "modern," art to private homes in this area came via Maruri-Weiss (the home of Tamargo's widow). The Edificio López Serrano (1932) is a magnificent example of a tall building designed in the Art Deco style. Principles of excellent construction techniques had been established, and municipal regulations were respected. During this period developers also followed both sets of standards, which guaranteed the prestige of El Vedado. In addition to the merits of its architecture and the metropolitan

Facing page: Edificio Triángulo, Calles 23 and 20, El Vedado; Cristóbal Díaz, architect.

Above: details of an apartment building (1930), Calles 11 and 4, El Vedado.

Left: private residence (1928), Calle 12, no. 407, El Vedado.

The tenants of an apartment hotel built by Castellá and Lecuona (engineers, architects, developers) on Calles 19 and 8, El Vedado, were almost able to drive their automobiles to the door of their rental housing. The building's appeal lay in the conveniences it offered. Its design was absolutely functional and promoted a practical aspect that included ornamentation such as bas-relief panels and voluminous flower vases made of molded cement, very popular at that time. The idea of apartment hotels was developed throughout this period, not only in El Vedado, but also in Centro Habana. The building (1941) (next page) was constructed on Calles 23 and G, El Vedado, and had an L-shaped layout, as per the design of the architect, Alejandro Capó, who incorporated already existing structures. The two unique entrances conferred a distinct character to the building and the two very simple friezes complement the building's rationalist approach.

feel of the zone, the area was also valued for being home to many important celebrities. Among them were Enrique García Cabrera, a distinguished painter and graphic artist, whose second home (1938) was built on Calle 22 and designed by the respected architect Max Borges del Junco. Its severe façade, marked by prominent pilasters, is enriched by the reliefs placed in the sections between the two floors. The upper reliefs were created by García Cabrera, and the lower by Manuel Rodulfo. The 1940s brought diverse ideas within the same "modern" style, that is, a considerable presence of architectural masses with

63

rounded angles. Apartment amenities included ample terraces instead of balconies. Exterior decoration was simple and well integrated into the general design. Two worthy examples are found in the buildings on the corner of Calle L and Calle 25.

Facing page: home of Enrique García Cabrera (1938) on Calle 22, El Vedado; Max Borges del Junco, architect.

Above: detail of the building on Calles O and 21, El Vedado.

Left: detail of the apartment building, Calles D and 17, El Vedado. Right: detail of the Rex apartment building, Calles J and 11, El Vedado.

From the town-planning standpoint, the upper-class neighborhood of El Vedado maintains features that are as evident on the exteriors of the building as within the confines established for the conduct of family life. The perfect correspondence between the structure of the facade and internal areas is evident in the Edificio Alemany (which bears the name of its architect-owner) whose massiveness leaves space for a doorway placed at the continuation of a short stairway that accentuates the elegant dignity achieved. It thereby follows the regulations for development under structural standards, the fruits of which are evident. In addition to the fine design of the vestibule floor, the superb quality of the stairway and its railing, with its stylizations of the traditional volutes so frequently found in Havana's colonial architecture, is notable.

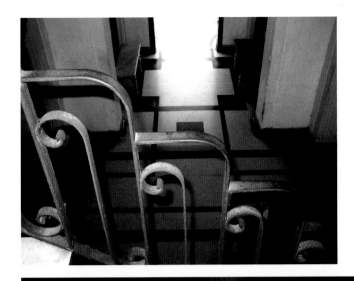

The central courtyard, a feature disappearing elsewhere in this urban setting, is to be found in this apartment house situated in a zone where there are several hospitals—also designed in Deco style. Here, the proportions are elongated in the manner of a hallway for all internal traffic, at the same time establishing a harmonious relationship between mass and empty spaces. It so integrates—organically—with the plan and the conception of the spaces that the desired environmental intimacy is bolstered, a happy conjunction in which new and traditional features appear to be perfectly coordinated.

HOSPITALS

The first large hospitals in the Deco style were initiated in 1930. These were two remarkable buildings on Calle G (Avenida de los Presidentes) in El Vedado: the Hospital Infantil Municipal and the Hospital Municipal de Maternidad. The Hospital de Maternidad Obrera in Marianao, which received the Gold Medal Award of the Colegio Nacional de Arquitectos in 1940, is also a leading design. The enormous scale of the structure, its excellent technical elements geared toward patient care, and the caliber of its design, place it among the finest institutional buildings in the country. Its façade, in which was placed a colossal sculpture by Teodoro Ramos Blanco—*Madre e Hijo*—has traits found in the Monumental Modern; while, in a harmonious combination of variations of the same style, its edges appear rounded, as in the Streamline. The building is a marvel of function, arranged in an arc with central and lateral projections. The vestibule design incorporates Vermont marble floors and plinth. It has an interesting circular shape whose space opens up through the three floors above; the stair banisters are made of chrome and the lighting is indirect. The surgery pavilion of the private clinic La Benéfica (c. 1942), designed by the architect José Antonio Vila, falls within the previously mentioned variation called Streamline. The rounded corners of its central base stand out in relation to the rest of the structure. La Benéfica was part of a complex of health institutions. This is one more example among the many buildings of this type that were defined stylistically through Art Deco.

Facing page: Clínica de Maternidad Obrera (1939), Marianao; Emilio de Soto, architect.

Below, left to right: two details of the Hospital Municipal de Maternidad (1930), Calles Línea and G, El Vedado; Evelio Govantes and Félix Cabarrocas, architects. Tower of the Hospital Militar, Marianao (1940), José Pérez Benitoa, architect. Crab by Rita Longa, façade of the Dispensario de la Liga Contra el Cancer; Leonardo Morales and Victor Morales, architects.

CHURCHES

"Modern" church buildings are linked to the development of suburban areas. The churches of San Agustín and Santa Rita, located in the suburbs of Nicanor del Campo and Miramar, respectively, are credited with breaking from the influence of the Neo-Gothic church design. Both were created by the architects Leonardo Morales and Victor Morales. The use of semielliptical parabolic arches made of reinforced concrete was a significant contribution to the structure, as were the labors of two "modern" Cuban sculptors, Juan José Sicre and Rita Longa. These two artists created, respectively, the Saint Augustine for the pediment of that church, and a plaster statue of Saint Rita, which was placed in the main altar of the second church. This came about after the Augustine priests, presided over by the Reverend Lorenzo Spiralli, had approved the modern designs. The subsequent polemic regarding the Art Deco image of Saint Rita, and whether or not it respected dogma, is an entirely different story. Another valuable contribution was the use of Cuban marble for part of the interior design. Carved elements in an openwork design facilitated the entry of air and natural light and achieved a beautiful decorative effect. The Iglesia Metodista y Centro Estudiantil Universitario is located in El Vedado. Constructed a decade after the others, it accomodates the uneven terrain through the use of an elevated flight of steps (as in San Agustín), a solution that created space for study halls. Protruding pilasters, the terraced architectural masses and its external decoration of light reliefs and openwork elements complete the exterior. The Colegio Nacional de Arquitectos named it the outstanding building of the year.

Previous and facing pages: Methodist Church and El Vedado University Student Center, Calles K and 25th, El Vedado; architect, Ricardo E. Franklin Acosta.

San Agustín Church, Calle 37 between Calles 42 and 44, Nicanor del Campo, Playa.

Noteworthy in the case of the two churches by the architects Morales—San Agustín and Santa Rita—is, first, the generosity of a devout member of the latter congregation, in donating the land needed for the construction and dedicating it to the memory of his mother. This gift made possible the presence of a highly distinctive work in this upscale neighborhood.

The Augustine fathers in charge of the churches in both Catholic centers were receptive, as we have indicated, to a renovating approach that would take into account the technical advances in ornamental elements that are organically related to the structural ones so outstanding in both cases. While certain similarity in the churches can be discerned, there are individual differences. There is, for example, the fact that Santa Rita stands virtually flush with beautiful Fifth Avenue (Avenida de las Americas) of Miramar, while San Agustín is set back an unusual distance from the relatively modest Nicanor del Campo street where it is located, seeking to join the evident monumentality of the religious aspect with modern architecture, of which it is representative at a high level. At the same time, the church maintains the traditional possibility of ornamentation of the domes created by the network of daring parabolic arches and takes advantage of those spaces for reasons—indubitably Art Deco—which careful restoration work keeps conveying in the coherence of the design. That criterion was retained also when contemporary craftsmen recently renovated the highly ornate stained-glass windows, which contributed considerably to the sumptuous ambience of the interior. The presence of modern plastic artists (Sicre in San Agustín, Rita Longa in Santa Rita) illustrated the practice existing at the time of enlisting artistic talent to function as artisans in construction.

In the Santa Rita Church the use of tiled roofing, a neocolonial feature,

could not neutralize the Deco character provided by the portico and sculptures of the façade. The two variants within a single poetic creation of the designers enhanced both the men's professional activity and the timeliness of the modern idiom in the context of the religious architecture of Havana.

MONUMENTAL MODERN STYLE

The building designed for the library of the Universidad de La Habana (1937) by the professor and architect Joaquín E. Weiss has a majestic elegance born of its classical interpretation in an Art Deco style known as Greco-Deco. Situated in a space bordering the Plaza Rector Cadenas (today known as the Plaza Ignacio Agramonte), it was meant to join a group of existing structures that comprised a renewal of historicist design. The architect created several porticos. The main portico, which opened out toward the square, is defined by tall pilasters whose capitals contain ornamentation that seems to echo Mesoamerican cultures. The second portico opens onto a side street, which runs in front of the Aula Magna and was designed by Weiss to become a reading and discussion area for students, as well as a waiting area for guests attending functions in the Aula. Thus, it is a building with two fronts sharing the same stylistic concept in spite of differences dictated by necessity. Communicative requirements were successfully resolved.

Both in its exterior and its interior, this building of brick and artificial stone veneers contains many remarkable decorations created by the architect and

Right: detail of an entrance to the Biblioteca de la Universidad de La Habana (1937); Joaquín E. Weiss, architect.

Following page: detail of the main portico of the Biblioteca de la Universidad de La Habana.

16

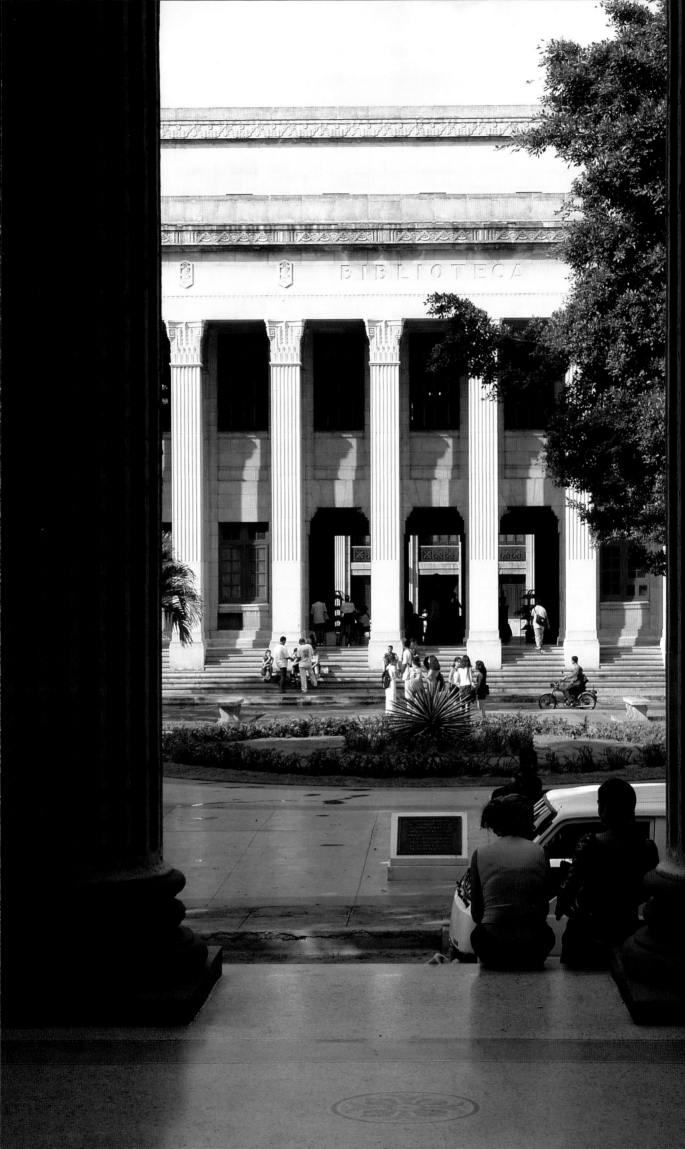

university professor Manuel Tapia Ruano. Adjoining the university campus is the stadium, a massive construction almost completely devoid of ornamentation, conceived in terms that fall well within the variety of Deco associated with the Monumental Modern. The revival of certain kinds of classical buildings is at the heart of what is known within Art Deco as Monumental Modern. Others, who prefer to interpret this style as a derivation rather than an organically related part of the style, use two words to label it: Modern Classical. This new version of the classical style within the Art Deco movement includes the use of porti-

Detail of the rear portico of the Biblioteca de la Universidad de La Habana.

cos whose supports, having neither bases nor capitals, surround an open area. Plaza Finlay, located between two important avenues in Marianao, the satellite city to the west, is bordered by four very similar buildings—the Centro Escolar, the Escuela del Hogar, the Escuela Normal de Kindergarten and the Asilo de Ancianos—that surround an obelisk. This central element is 32 meters (105 feet) high, with a black granite base topped with a frieze carved by the sculptors Navarro and Lombardo. A hard stone shaft rises above the frieze and is crowned by a lantern that serves as a beacon for airplanes. As an integrated complex, the Plaza is the most notable example of the variation found here and was designed by the architect José Pérez Benitoa.

During the 1940s two subtly different buildings were constructed. One was designed by Govantes and Cabarrocas for the Biblioteca de la Sociedad Económica de Amigos del País. In addition to the reading room and library proper, the building includes offices and an auditorium for cultural events and the institution's functions. The problem of creating a multifunctional building was resolved through the habitual skills of its creators. However, since Félix Cabarrocas was also an excellent sculptor, the hand of the plastic artist is quite visible in the sculptural accents that flank the entrance and in the vestibule design. The architect Manuel Tapia Ruano was also a gifted sculptor. This is immediately apparent in the Escuela de Veterinaria of the Universidad de La Habana. The four stone pilasters that define the elevated portico of the main entrance are crowned by carved horse heads, while feline figures are incorporated into

Rear façade of the Biblioteca de la Universidad de La Habana.

their bases and reinforce their application in the façade. The angular layout of the structure is a result of an intelligent use of the land necessitated by the building's multifunctional nature. The treatment accorded the internal spaces received the same attention as its exterior details.

Facing page: Escuela de Veterinaria of the Universidad de La Habana (1943), Ayestarán and Carlos III; Manuel Tapia Ruano, architect.

Above: Biblioteca de la Sociedad Económica de Amigos del País (1945); Evelio Govantes and Félix Cabarrocas, architects.

Left: detail of the Biblioteca de la Sociedad Económica de Amigos del País. Center: Obelisco in Plaza Finlay (1944), Marianao; José Pérez Benitoa, architect. Right: detail of the Obelisco.

Constraints of physical space prompted shifting to lands farther away from the deanery and the neighboring Rector Cadenas Plaza of the University of Havana, to meet the need for proper accommodations, which would be conceived, from the stylistic standpoint, as variants of Monumental Modern. The School of Dentistry (at Carlos III and Zapata) was built from a 1943 plan by Esteban Rodríguez Castells, who designed the Edificio Bacardi. This great architect was able to find a way to introduce sites for university specialties into the overall plan through formal features that differed radically from his prior practices Other outstanding examples are the Chemistry School (at Zapata near G), with a monumental stairway that simultaneously separates the building from, and connects it to, the street; likewise, the Medical School (at Calle 25 in El Vedado) is approached by a grand stairway, although one radically different from that of the Chemistry School. The latter is a building further distinguished by its sharply accented verticality and by a purity of line that shows off the surprising accent of an ornamental cast concrete plaque within the extremely austere overall composition of the main façade.

STREAMLINE

The economic crisis of 1929 marked the beginning of a period of austerity in the United States. It was essential to reduce construction costs, and Streamline clearly reflects these conditions. Similarly, it expressed a desire for renewal through simpler forms. The image of velocity and all things industrial are distinctive traits found in surfaces that alternate between planes and curves. The function of the nautical variation of the style is part of the same conceptual framework. The Edificio Solimar presents conscious adaptations to climate and to the trapezoidal shape of the site. The curved, rhythmic balconies of its façade have windows on two sides, providing access to natural light and ventilation as well as facilitating the building's internal flow of traffic. On the other hand, the only entrance to this simply designed building reflects a generous decorative sense: an old-fashioned wrought-iron and glass confection.

Facing page: Edificio Solimar (1944), Calles Soledad and San Lázaro, Centro Habana; Manuel Copado, architect.

This page: nautical elements in the details of a residence, Calle Juan Bruno Zayas, Reparto La Víbora.

General design elements of the Art Deco Streamline style were creatively used in Havana. This is demonstrated in the rounded corners of walls as well as in the use of eaves (fluid bands that connoted velocity); the level tops of buildings, finished in uniform parapets; the horizontal disposition and geometric frame of windows; and the use of limestone for details. The use of balconies and terraces reminiscent of ship decks together with the metallic bands used in railings were assimilated by the architectural style of Miami Beach's South Beach. They are also found in Havana's housing and public buildings. Portholes, also often present, accentuate the nautical feel of some structures, a feature dictated by spatial function.

The Gran Templo Masónico is a distant heir of Streamline. More typical examples of this style are the car dealerships and auto-parts shops that dot the streets from Calle Humboldt and Calle Hospital, to Calle 25 and Calle Hospital, in the neighborhood of Cayo Hueso, Centro Habana. The clean, rounded shapes of the constructions, their fluid bands and horizontally placed windows, clearly express function and design. Here we see how limited resources are rescued by the clarity of the architectural lexicon, which evokes a change in esthetic values through the whole of its component parts. The architect Críspulo Goizueta conceived the Residencias Cantera (1940–1941) on the corner of Infanta and Humboldt. For a long time this project was thought to have been designed by Esteban Rodríguez Castells. In reality, it was Goizueta who created it for the architectural company co-owned by Rodríguez Castells. The two-story building emphasizes the horizontal. Among the few ornamental details are geometric designs that serve as access signs and which are found in the terrazzo floors of the portal, and an arrangement of balconies containing rounded borders and eaves. The efficient austerity of its contributing elements served its function well: to provide a block of apartments for middle-class families of some means who wished to live comfortably in a well-situated neighborhood.

Left: Gran Templo Nacional Masónico (1951–1955), Calles Carlos III and Belascoaín, Centro Habana; Emilio Vasconcelos, architect. Center: detail of the façade's clock. Right: the building's crown.

The building on the corner of Calle Belascoaín (today known as Padre Varela) and the Avenida de Carlos III (today known as Salvador Allende) was constructed for the Gran Templo Nacional Masónico of the Gran Logia of Cuba of A.L. and A.M. (meaning Antiguos, Libres and Aceptados Masones—Ancient, Free and Accepted Masons). The first stone was placed at a ceremony during which earth brought from all areas of Cuba was deposited. That earth was sprinkled with water from the largest rivers of each province. Difficulties due to the settling of the land caused a long construction period that lasted four years. The date of its completion demonstrates the permanence of the style in Cuba. Here the influence of Streamline, a variant of Art Deco, is expressed, for example, in its rounded corners.

It is interesting to note that even within the general features that characterize the variant Streamline style, there are special structural details worthy of consideration. The curved elements that appear to be balconies and to delineate the façade of the Edificio Solimar are, in fact, passageways that allow access to the front doors of the apartments, while the actual balconies are arranged along the rear façade of the building. This factor contributes substantially to the creative design solutions applied in an avant-garde mode within the town-planning canon; the unusual insertion of curves contrasts with the rectilinear design of the neighboring buildings. Various functions were served on the basis of the more or less consistent adaptation of the curved element as in the Cine Astral on Calle Infanta, built with the distinctive corner panel designed to employ glass blocks and crowned with a graceful cornice. That element, side by side with oculi, speaks for the character of this variant in a building that also includes apartment units in the design of a movie theater, a favorite Deco subject.

The Residencias Cantera building is introduced into a zone characterized by its stylistic coherence.

THE CEMETERY

The construction of the Cementerio Cristóbal Colón in Havana took place at the conclusion of a contest held in 1869 in which the winner was the Spaniard Calixto de Loira. This necropolis covers approximately 50 hectares (123.55 acres) of land west of the city, in El Vedado. The cemetery is archetypal, given the quantity and quality of its monuments. Foreign and Cuban artists contributed to the splendor that gave solace to the long departed—if, of course, they had the means to pay for it. Over the years, exquisite materials were used, such as sumptuous granites, Italian marble, and marble extracted from the best Cuban quarries, which resulted in headstones and monuments of great beauty. This constitutes an authentic outdoor museum that displays a large inventory of designs. Without a doubt, Art Deco, with its solid roots in the national context, could not fail to be present. The octagon, favored in large-scale Art Deco structures, forms the basis for the simple mausoleum dedicated to the sugar magnate Andrés Gómez Mena. Its early construction (1920) places it at the head of the roster of pioneering designs. Among other valuable works is the outstanding tomb of Catalina Lasa. Juan Pedro Baró, her widower, commis-

Facing page: Catalina Lasa–Juan Pedro Baró mausoleum (1936); René Lalique, designer.

Below, left to right: entrance to the Catalina Lasa–Pedro Baró mausoleum; lateral view of the Catalina Lasa–Pedro Baró mausoleum; Andrés Gómez Mena pantheon (ca. 1930), Frank Steinhart pantheon (ca. 1937).

Many of the mausoleums are chapels, large enough for several visitors. Valuable decorations such as stained-glass windows and bas-reliefs elevate the importance of these monuments. The latter ornamentation almost always appears in the exterior, as in *La ascención* (1937), created by the Cuban Juan José Sicre for the Frank Steinhart vault. The addition of authentic works of art makes these structures more interesting.

Left: Prío Socarrás family mausoleum. Center: Domingo León vault. Right: Falla Bonet family vault.

Carlos Miguel de Céspedes vault.

sioned the designer René Lalique in 1936. At the white marble and black granite entrance, two carved angels pray beneath a small cross. The mass of the entrance is octagonal. The apse-shaped chapel appears to be perforated by crystal-covered squares. The rose motif can be found in glass design elements in the chapel's interior. This motif brings to mind the creation of the flower named after the deceased. Another monument in the Deco style that merits attention is dedicated to the memory of the Veteranos de las Guerras de Independencia. It dates from 1945, and the architect in charge, Luis Dauval, based it on an original design by Enrique Luis Varela. The reliefs created by the sculptors Florencio Gelabert and Juan José Sicre were important in the design of the mausoleum. The stone walls and the bronze of the sculptured pieces establish a strong sculptural contrast. The analysis of how this necropolis successfully integrated the basic principles of this style demonstrates the influence of the highly aware upper-class families of Cuban society, who had an interest in keeping abreast of the latest world fashions and were intent on upholding—in the best possible way—a high standard of living, even beyond death. The architecture and sculptures found in the many extraordinary monuments admired here once again affirm the deep roots of Art Deco in the Cuban capital.

Detail of the mausoleum of the Veteranos de las Guerras de Independencia (ca.1945); Enrique Luis Varela and Luis Dauval, architects; Florencio Gelabert and Juan José Sicre, sculptors.

INTERIORS
AND FURNITURE

INTERIORS AND FURNITURE

In terms of home design, the most controlled organic spaces to have survived can be found in the Catalina Lasa mansion, shown in the photographs at the opening of this chapter. This home, created as a backdrop for a couple who, as members of the elite bourgeoisie, had ample resources at their disposal, is clearly an exceptional case. It was not the typical environment of the newly rich, since it broke with the prevailing drive to acquire objects of the most varied origins. The estate is the embodiment of the principles of Art Deco regarding the creation of an environment whose components flow in the same direction. Catalina Lasa's friends surely questioned her sanity when she selected her home décor, since she had had the option of choosing from the world's greatest antique galleries. Nothing that could interfere with the house's stylistic harmony—including paintings—was incorporated into the environment. The distribution of space, the use of the most advanced lighting techniques, the wall finishes, the elimination of rugs and the ensuing splendor of bare floors, along with the simple lines of the furniture, would result in an excellent example of Art Deco.

At the time, it was an accepted fact that substantial resources were not invested in "modern" mansions. This was not true for blocks of apartments or public buildings. Moreover, it is necessary to think about how the spaces created during this period were affected by the passage of time, lack of care, or ignorance. The house of the painter and talented graphic artist Enrique García Cabrera, also in El Vedado, is on an entirely different level and not comparable to the splendor of the mansion on Paseo and Calle 17. This home, preserved and maintained by his descendants, is outstanding for its strict stylistic interior design. An article in *Interiores Modernos* (May 1931) about the Álvarez Sánchez home in El Vedado—Ernesto Batista, architect; Clara Porset, interior designer—describes how interior design was conceived and what was contained within the framework of the period. Clara Porset, wrote: "The present-day decorative movement exhibits characteristics opposed to Art Nouveau. There is nothing more reflective, logical, balanced or harmonious than the expression of Modern Art." This is apparent in the arrangement of the furniture, made of gray sycamore and other neutral tones, and the strict geometric design of the floor. The focus of this simply designed room is a screen made of bronze inlay created by the Cuban artist Mario Carreño (who at the time signed as Karreño). This introduced an important element, a nexus between the creators of the artistic vanguard and those of decorative works. The work cannot be considered an example of a common style, since it is found in an upper-class private residence. Nonetheless, these advanced ideas had penetrated this level of design. The writing of Berta A. Martínez-Márquez reflected this notion in December of 1929 when she wrote about the renowned French designer Émile-Jacques Ruhlmann: "We have repeated it often: the new art has marked its path in interior design." Her opinion was supported by works such as the Art Deco design created by the architect César F. Guerra for the Sixth Pan-American Conference (1928). The design, exhibited in the Aula Magna of the Universidad de La Habana, surely clashed violently with the historicist style of the outstanding framework within which it was placed. Moreover, some excellent examples survive today, especially in apartment buildings and public buildings. Here the "new" is imprinted on significant parts of interior spaces such as vestibules. All of the elements of interior design were integrated into the lobby of the grand Edificio López Serrano, which still boasts of a brilliant stylistic coherence. The small vestibule of the apartment tower of the Edificio Rodríguez Vázquez, on Galiano, between Concordia and Neptuno, highlights the quality of its design, apparent in its excellent black and white terrazzo floors as well as its iron scrollwork. There are other similar examples, where the original layout of the components can still be appreciated.

The range covered here is as vast as the interpretations of Art Deco, adaptations suited to the physical and intellectual conditions of all things Cuban. Here the style was used not only in façades but also incorporated in interiors, where there was always room for reality and fantasy.

EDIFICIO EMILIO BACARDÍ

The Edificio Emilio Bacardí is characterized by the richness of the materials used in constructing both its exterior and its interior. On the façade one finds Labrador and red Bavarian granite, which changes to a rose hue in the principal vestibule. Here, a soft green marble was used for the first time in Cuba, and black and white veined marble covers the walls of its two lobbies from floor to ceiling. According to the suppliers of the exquisite stone destined for this building, the Edificio Bacardí boasted marble and granite from across Europe: Germany, Sweden, Norway, Italy, France, Belgium and Hungary. Geometrized natural elements, a basic solution to the ornamental dictates developed in Art Deco, appear with obsessive frequency in the interior of the building. Zigzags and triangles are constants in the ceiling stucco as well as in the floors. The volute, an obvious link with plant themes, is the main motif of the grilles used on doors, windows and other openings. It was also applied to the design of the great stained-glass window at the end of the vestibule, where etched opaque glass

The majestic exterior of the building is complemented by its interior. Marble, granite, glass, lamps, stucco and ironwork express a kind of brilliant *horror vacui*, part of the conceptual drive for strict design control. The generous use of color as well as abundant ornamentation resulted in a lasting tribute to the style. The applied concept corresponds completely to the way in which interior architecture was envisioned at the time. Located in a densely populated area of the city's historic center, the doors of the Edificio Bacardí are open to permanent contact with the urban milieu.

Edificio Emilio Bacardí: paint, marquetry and gold leaf were combined for the design on the doors of the bar restrooms.

Keyhole with bat, a recurring motif.

The principal vestibule, the mezzanine bar, and the exhibition hall contain sumptuous ornamentation that fills all of the available space. Palm motifs are used to bring a tropical accent to the space and are included in the decoration of the bar restrooms, while the surfaces of the elevator doors have a carved radial sun design. The present-day look of these interiors is the result of an important restoration project—directed by the Oficina del Historiador de la Ciudad—which has returned the building to its former splendor. All of the woodwork was done in valuable Cuban wood—mahogany and cedar—by the firm of Pi y Brioso S.A.; the workshops of Duque y Compañía were responsible for the plasterwork. La Insular, a national factory specializing in bronze and wrought-iron lamps, did custom work for the project, and the Venetian shutters found throughout the building were made by the firm Argenta, also Cuban. Wrought-iron and bronze fences were made by the Cerrajería Artística Basora, in the "modern decorative style." The Graysna Company of Wunsiedel, Bavaria, in charge of the construction work, completes the roster of national and foreign collaborators responsible for carrying out this ambitious project, which was made possible by the great talent of its many Cuban technicians and workers.

and amber-colored glass were used. The design of the sun's rays is repeated on the marble mosaic floor and on the elevator doors. In the exhibition hall the stuccoed capitals of its attached pilasters, as well as its frieze panels, repeat the rose pattern. The panels also depict fruit bowls with pineapples as a tropical accent. Mirrors, gold, and pastel shades define this space, and elegance and good taste unify the complex design; all these elements project an image of unique splendor.

Above: stucco ceiling in the exhibition hall of the Edificio Emilio Bacardí.

Left: elevator door of the Edificio Emilio Bacardí.

The area designated for the bar of the Edificio Bacardi appealed in a special way to the designers' creativity, good taste and budgetary concerns. This testified to the fact that no lesser modality, earmarked as a complement to the main work, the building itself, would, in its all-embracing reality, be considered minor or of lesser importance. This relatively small space, available as a mezzanine on the two sides that open towards the showroom on the ground floor, is rich without being ostentatious, unifying in its arrangement of the many elements in play, superbly functional and—let us say so without hesitation—true to the profession of faith in Deco which permeates the building as a whole. This quality can be observed, as well, in the fixtures and lamps, the rectilinear design of the terrazzo floor, the walls lined with maple bark, the intricate decoration of the doors to the restrooms, and the elegant outline of the bar used to serve the magnificent rum produced by the company that financed the building. It is worth the trouble to analyze the concept of the openings that offer a splendid view of the main floor and the street. The fine design of the furniture and the attention to detail is also evident in the angle of the galloon (one of the Deco motifs par excellence) on the bases of the little tables. Nothing was left to chance in the conception and creation of an atmosphere intended to transform a meeting place of artists and notables, national and foreign, desiring to enjoy what is know as "class," to enhance the charm of a special encounter.

CATALINA LASA'S HOME

The home the sugar magnate Juan Pedro Baró built for Catalina Lasa is exceptional for two reasons: the quality of its design and the events that surrounded the couple. The gardens, created by Lemón, Legriñá y Compañía—the best landscapers in Havana—were based on a concept by J. C. N. Forestier, known as "the wizard of the parks." Stucco walls and columns came from Dominique's of Paris. The rarest and most beautiful Italian marbles were chosen, such as Portoro gold and Siena yellow among others, which, as the reviewer Renée de García Kohly noted in 1930 "create a dazzling carpetlike effect throughout the house with their beautiful, bright colors integrated in a truly artistic manner." The steps at the entrance, made of red Languedoc marble, lead to a wrought-iron door designed superbly by Baguez of Paris, which also created the grates for the house. Sand from the Nile River and excellent Cuban wood, such as mahogany, were used extensively throughout the house. It is generally known that René Lalique was involved in the interior design. Luis Estévez Lasa, the eldest son from Catalina Lasa's first marriage, created the furniture found in the great room, where the marble, stucco and indirect lighting create a special atmosphere. However, "the dining room is the *clou* [star attraction] of the house, given its originality and style."

The white marble dining table, bordered in yellow with a central mirror inlay, was built in situ. The chairs are made of yellow sycamore and cushioned in horsehair of the same color. The corners of the room hold glass cases with mirrored backs "in which one can observe delicate crystal flowers from the renowned House of Chanel." A single marble step leads to *la serre*, a sort of greenhouse with Lalique glass panes and views of the garden. Its floors are made of silver and green-turquoise ceramic tiles, at the center of which is a water fountain. All of the spaces received special consideration and care. Thus, the sun porch or "winter garden" has masonry walls covered in finely carved woodwork, and a square-lantern-shaped planter, designed to brim with flowers, hangs from the vaulted ceiling over the central fountain.

Considered a great beauty in her time, Catalina Lasa had been married to Luis Estévez, the son of the vice president of the Republic of Cuba. During a ball organized in her own home, she met the millionaire Juan Pedro Baró. They fell in love, and shortly afterward she left her husband for him.

Scandal erupted and the most highly placed families of the city ostracized the lovers. One evening the couple attended a function at the Teatro National. The audience—wishing to torment the pair—abandoned the theater, thus leav-

Planter lamp in the sun room, home of Catalina Lasa.

ing them alone. This situation forced the couple to leave Havana for Paris, where detectives contracted by the Estévez family would continue to hound them. They then sought a papal audience in Rome and obtained the annulment of the first marriage. Catalina followed Juan to Venice and they married in 1917. This passionate relationship was reflected in the magnificent mansion Juan Pedro Baró built for his beloved and in a series of events that included the creation of a rose named after Catalina Lasa. She died in Paris on November 3, 1930. Her body was embalmed and buried—with a rose in her hands—in the beautiful mausoleum designed by Lalique in Havana's Cementerio de Cristóbal Colón.

Transom window in the covered porch of the Catalina Lasa home.

FURNITURE

The interior designer Teodoro Bailey, who was partial to historicist styles, wrote, first in July of 1926 and then later in May of 1927, ". . . Modern Art is not based on any prior style. On the contrary, its creators have tried to design objects which are as apart as possible from all previously known styles." What he found objectionable was precisely what Art Deco contributed to the art of design; in this light Art Deco was valued by the developing cultural movement in the capital. The widespread use of Deco furniture throughout Cuba is surprising, particularly within a population of modest means. The stepped design of some buildings was adapted to the outline of the furniture pieces while geometric patterns were carved on surfaces. One must remember that these were the work of simple artisans who sold pieces out of their own homes or in modest furniture stores. Thus the small scale of the pieces destined for the living room, the dining room or the bedroom. Naturally, the large establishments created—for those who could afford them—imposing furniture in the European style, albeit designed and made in Cuba. The only luxury granted to

Facing page: nickel silver panel designed by Enrique García Cabrera in the vestibule of the Edificio López Serrano.

Above and left: dining room set with typical Cuban mahogany pieces. Sideboard and glass case, essential furnishings in the Cuban home.

Facing page: entrance foyer in the home of Enrique García Cabrera, where one can appreciate the ingenious furniture-door to the guest bathroom.

Left to right above: another view of the stairway and bar in the home of Enrique García Cabrera.

On the following two pages: Enrique García Cabrera's studio-parlor.

Cuban Deco furniture was the use of beautiful and precious woods, particularly mahogany, which was strong enough to withstand termites. The ingenuity of the carpenters facilitated the continuing tradition of adapting historical styles to climate. This was accomplished via the substitution of open, cool wickerwork for cushions and upholstery. In this simple, clever way, Cuban furniture integrated "modern" decoration and elegance without sacrificing comfort. The interior design architect Clara Porset clearly stated the following principle: "We would have to adopt, not precisely new forms, since the modern spirit is the same everywhere and identical principles propel us; but at least a variation of materials that would be suited to the climate." An important concept in the analysis of the evolution of Art Deco furniture is how it accentuates architectural and sculptural features.

The criteria for this emphasis is that the furniture must share the architecture's essential characteristics, that its essence be transformed from mobile (random, changing) to immobile; that is, to an integrated part of the space in which it is found, as a whole conceived by the creator of the entire project rather than merely an added-on decorator's idea. The expanding scope of furniture is a significant aspect of these changes, especially when the furnishings

114

become a more integrated part of the whole. The invention of the radio, a medium of information and the culture representative of this era, forced the need for ad hoc designs for this novelty in the modern home. This—as happened with the television later—became the focal point of the living room. Another example is the dressing table—the "boudoir" of modest homes—which appeared constantly among furnishings, as did the decorative screens used to define spaces. These changes extended to utilitarian rooms such as the kitchen and bathroom, or invaded public establishments (bars, ice cream parlors, restaurants, flower shops) with large, stationary furniture such as that found in the bar

Facing page: mahogany armchair; anonymous designer.

Left: dressing table in rare Cuban wood; anonymous designer.

Lluvia de Oro situated on Calle Obispo in Old Havana. The artist Enrique García Cabrera, a subject of great interest to the media, provided a good example of this new concept for the design of living space. Using text and images, an entire page in *Alturas de Almendares* was dedicated to describing his first home, which illustrates his influence. When he designed his new home in El Vedado—already well within the new style—he directly intervened in specific design areas, such as the furniture for his study and the bar. Such involvement resulted in a home that reflects the nuances of his personality. Metal furniture was considered "a typical product of the industrial arts of our time, due to the use it is subjected to;" but we believe that as a rule, such furnishings were used in businesses or health facilities, where their practicality was unquestioned. However, such furniture was destined to occupy open or semiopen spaces when used in

Below: top left: detail of an armoire; bottom left: glass case with acid-etched ornamentation; right: furniture designed by Jaime Valls for his study.

Facing page: mahogany bar, from La Lluvia de Oro, Calle Obispo, no. 316, corner of Havana, Old Havana.

housing. An advertisement from 1932 for Gaubeca y Ucelay S.A. announced the sale of "modern steel furniture" manufactured exclusively for front porches.

However, two factors may have undermined its popularity: a prejudice among homeowners because it represented a clear break from wood furniture; and cost, since the metals used, whether bronze, steel, copper or iron, required nickel or chrome plating and were quite expensive.

Left and below: wrought-iron console and table with marble and crystal tops, respectively. Jardín Casa Trías, El Vedado.

Facing page: built-in console in the dining room of the López Chávez home, Reparto Kohly.

When deciding on the furniture for Deco spaces, different ideas might arise in buildings designed for different purposes and with varying levels of luxury. For example, the house in El Vedado planned by the architect Emilio Vasconcelos for himself, the living room (still kept in exceptional condition by Alicia Pérez Malo, the daughter-in-law of the original owner) demonstrates the characteristic rigor of the style, with the furniture of upholstered wood matching the vertical bands on the stucco wall, and the synthetic forms of the side tables. Such design choices are a good example of what was considered comfort when the house was built in 1938.

The School of Gastroenterology preserves examples of wooden furniture designed especially for the school, as well as for the reception area, a kind of a roofed pavilion, an accent of exceptional quality that lightens the seriousness of the atmosphere. A marble bench with very ornate legs authenticates this type of movable-immovable furniture that was to establish the mode of utilization of common spaces, as seen even today in the Edificio Alemany. The purpose of this particularization is to reveal creative variants through very simple solutions which, however, clearly reveal prevailing concepts when it comes to furnishing a space.

BATHROOMS

The bathroom is a private, practical space par excellence that could not be treated indifferently, particularly at a time when comfort and hygiene were important goals for builders at all income levels. There is a kind of bath that was designed on a more formal line, called at that time a bath-boudoir. This was designed by a decorator who, in spite of the ornamental nature of the work, had to consider materials as well as fixtures and their practical uses. Another purely functional kind of bathroom was solely the architect's responsibility: it had solid fixtures devoid of decoration and was designed around the use of waterproof materials and shiny metals that encased mirrors and doors, thus completing the finishing touches on an essentially "modern" space. Additionally, recommendations were made concerning the way areas were to be divided and how best to provide adequate ventilation for sanitary reasons.

Facing page: bathroom-boudoir in the mansion of Maria Luisa Gómez Mena, Countess Revilla de Camargo (today the Museo de Artes Decorativas), Calles 17 and E, El Vedado.

The supply of bathroom appliances and tiles was guaranteed by accredited firms such as Mott-Pons y Pons, and Cobo y Compañía, both of which had exhibit and salesrooms in the capital. The variety of the designs carried out in these materials is noteworthy, a credit to the imagination of their creators. These are functional bathrooms, endowed with the best technical elements and sometimes embellished with striking stained glass.

FLOORING

Stucco and floor treatments were two very important elements in Art Deco because of their great decorative effect. While stucco has a grand tradition from its use in earlier styles, it can be said that Art Deco used it to its greatest advantage. There are numerous examples of the extensive use of stucco on ceilings, cornices and decorative soffits. These designs were combined with friezes and borders of varied motifs that ran through sections of wall, thereby elevating their importance. In addition, stucco was applied to change the surface of columns and walls. It is found in abundant variety in different kinds of structures: in private homes, of course, but also in apartment and public buildings, as important accents to the architectural environment.

Some notable and highly sophisticated examples can be seen in the vestibules of the Biblioteca de la Sociedad Económica de Amigos del País and in the Escuela de Veterinaria of the Universidad de La Habana. Floor design was prominent in Cuban Art Deco, an extremely important element in a country whose climate made

carpeting or rugs unnecessary. Floor tiles, terrazzo, granite, and marble made in Cuba or elsewhere were common in areas where designers played an important role.

The architects of the "new" art explored the potential of this factor in order to assert that all was under control. Floor tiles were used extensively in apartments and in private residences, while terrazzo, granite and marble were used in the great mansions and public buildings. Abstract, animal, plant and historical motifs were developed in flooring that largely surpassed its humble function. Here are found the rhythmic triangles that became directional access signs (Cine Fausto), an entire zodiac in the foyer of the Cine-Teatro América, and the electrifying concentric bolts of lightning that grace the Sanatorio Infantil Antituberculoso La Esperanza. These structures exemplify the opulent inventory still standing proudly, testaments to the important design aspects of Art Deco.

The concept of big houses and apartment buildings included the exclusive design of harmonious pavements in tune with the overall plan.

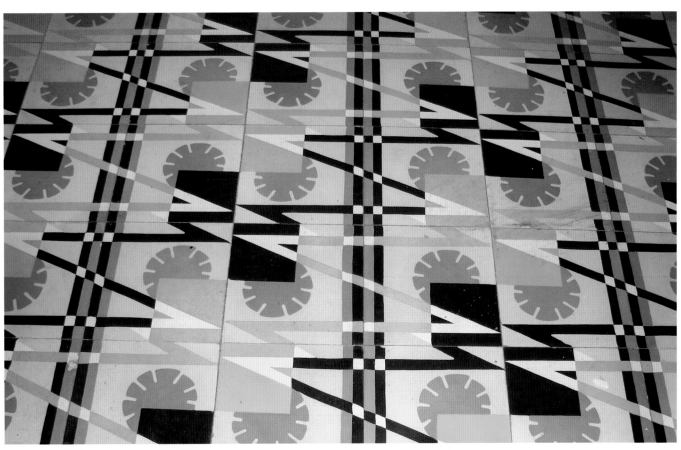

STAIRWAYS

Stairways—three-dimensional zigzags—were developed in ways that high-lighted the buildings of this period. These broadly followed the particular nuances of the variants adopted in the style. Stairways emphasized the spaces in which they were situated, combining their proper function with a sculptural and more decorative role. They ranged from stairways designed according to a more rectilinear form, in which the geometry of the metal created transparent surfaces, to the more substantial ones, where architectural mass acquired a significant sculptural importance. The stairway, a predominant factor in many

Facing page: detail of the stairway of the apartment building Alemany, Calle 13 between Calles 14 and 16, El Vedado.

Below: detail of the stairway of the Hilda Sarrá residence (1934), Calles 2 and 19, El Vedado. Today, it is the Casa del Festival del Nuevo Cine Latinoamericano.

homes, would play a special role in the construction of public buildings and apartment buildings.

Within another domain of decoration—that of interior architecture—this design feature was used extensively because of the fact that, even without being a structural element, it is essentially tectonic. Once constructed, a staircase

Facing page: bottom of a stairway, apartment building at Calles F and 25, El Vedado.

Left: bird's-eye view of the same stairway.

Left: another angle of the same stairway. Center: stairway in the home of Catalina Lasa. Right: stairway in the López Chávez residence.

Following page: stairway in the Colegio Nacional de Arquitectos.

cannot be removed at whim. Surely its static nature has saved it from substantial transformation and ensured that these stairways have survived to date in generally pristine condition. Thus, the presence of stairways serves as a permanent sculptural tribute to the glory of ornamentation.

Stairways, an important element in the definition of interior space, retained the monumental character typical of the previous historicist styles. In this manner they preserved their significance while developing great freedom in terms of form. The lobby of the Colegio Nacional de Arquitectos is a magnificent example of the relationship between stairways and natural and artificial lighting.

MOLDINGS

Stucco, the means for obtaining an aesthetic impression of, say, "a shell-like coating," offers nearly ideal possibilities to the plasterers who skillfully contributed to the cohesion of the interior spaces. The material's plasticity, economy, and other qualities were utilized in an ongoing, creative manner to showcase the broad range of Deco's decorative repertoire. Hallways, living rooms, private or public areas were given accents aimed at emphasizing the professed stylistic intentions, and imbuing all available space with an artistic character. Many highly skilled Catalonian artisans arrived in Cuba during the early twentieth century, among them a large number of plasterers. The rapidly popularized technique adopted by locals led to the realization of a wide range of motifs that adorned walls and ceilings, without ignoring the possibilities of masking the indirect light sources or the option of lending an interesting appearance to certain particularly unattractive surfaces. Major assignments, such as that taken on by the firm Duque y Compañía for the great Edificio Bacardí project, yielded considerable results in both the foyer of the building and the showroom. A particularly outstanding example can likewise be seen in the lobby of the Edificio López Serrano. In both places we found that it competes on an equal footing with many finer and more-expensive materials such as marble and granite. The use of stucco in the design of major works was unlimited: detail, the plain frieze, the

austere accentuation of a column or the discrete entablature provided a welcome opportunity for the craftsmen to add luster to the overall project or merely to satisfy the well-intentioned wish of the modest investor to be fashionable.

LIGHTING

In a 1929 article the Cuban architect J. M. Bens Arrate referred to the work created by a French expert when he wrote about how "modern" lighting required more or less veiled sources of various intensities and colors in order to prevent damage to the eye. He was also concerned with the correct placement of lamps, later referring to the use of soffits, appliqués, wall sconces, and lights that appeared to emerge from the floor or were placed in vases, screens and other works of art. He concluded that in the long run indirect lighting, a product of the era, had been the most developed. He advocated the use of diffused lighting and a touch of the theatrical when incorporating this element. In general, the debate regarding the use of lighting seemed to center on whether or not

The use of molding and lead resulted in a wide range of designs for stained-glass windows, which filtered natural light sources.

lighting should be considered as important a functional-decorative factor as any other design component in a room. This involved not only the logical design of artificial sources of light, but also the appropriate use of natural light. This debate occurred during a time when people began to focus more on practical consideration, such as comfort, hygiene, and other important aspects of "modern" life. The recommended solutions included the creation of many windows with milky glass to filter the intensity of the sun's rays; the creation of surfaces covered by etched glass bricks, which were frequently used—especially in public structures—to cover considerable wall space.

This latter element created a distinguishable stylistic trait. Also used were options such as round glass skylights etched with still-lifes, landscapes or abstract designs. Reflective lamps, which beamed light toward the ceiling and cre-

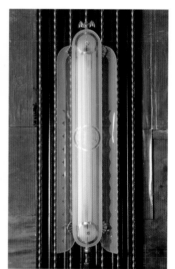

Ceiling light and wall sconce in the Edificio Bacardí.

Ceiling lights from the home of Catalina Lasa.

Sitting room of an apartment—currently used as a hairdresser's—located on Calle San Miguel, no. 106, Centro Habana.

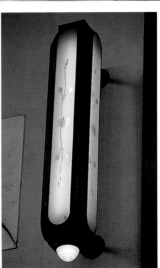

One of the most common ceiling lamp designs.

The "veiling" of light was a conscious objective artfully expressed and maintained even in the most capricious designs. The new concept of using light as an important decorative factor while retaining its function was thus reinforced. Milky glass and either acid-etched or sandblasted glass added a sensual beauty to an ultimately functional goal through this charming ornamentation.

Wall lamp in the church of San Antonio de Padua, Quinta Avenida and Calle 60, Miramar.

ated sufficient illumination from the rebounding rays, were favored in design. Also favored were bands of translucent glass which, placed in ceiling borders or in specific areas, disguised a room's sources of light. While panels made of plaster or other materials were used with great effect, the placement of electric lightbulbs, either behind these designs or in the path of natural light, elevated the stature of lighting design. This was a matter of usefulness combined with ornamentation.

Facing page: lounge area of the women's restroom in the Cine-Teatro América.

Below: lounge area of the gentlemen's restroom in the Cine-Teatro América. Right, foreground: a lamp used to illuminate the area with light reflected from the ceiling.

Following pages: Cine-Teatro América

CINE-TEATRO AMÉRICA

Indirect lighting is important with respect to the definition of spaces in the Cine-Teatro América. The use of this element is evident in the spaciousness of the lobby, which boasts a stupendous terrazzo floor with zodiac motifs, and in the hallways and waiting areas. All of this, along with alternatives such as the cushioning of walls, the use of leather, mirrors and an effective overall placement of decorative elements, make this theater a significant example of a design concept that underscores the treatment of all elements of interior architecture as equally important. A company run by an Italian family, Gottardi, made the curtains and upholstery. The waiting area that leads to the women's lounge was designed in theatrical terms. Subsequent renovations have obliterated certain details, but the style was essentially preserved.

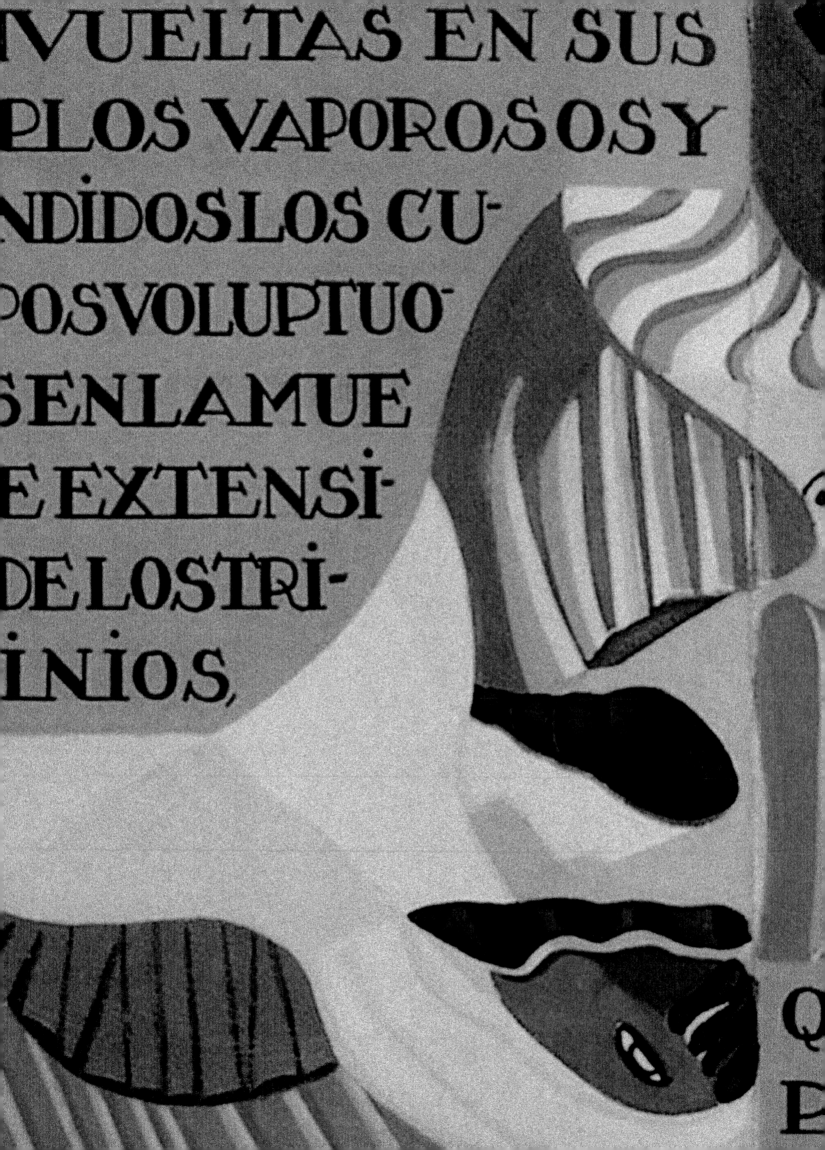

VUELTAS EN SUS
PLOS VAPOROSOS Y
NDIDOS LOS CU-
POS VOLUPTUO-
SEN LA MUE
E EXTENSI-
DE LOS TRI-
INIOS.

VISUAL ARTS

VISUAL ARTS

During the period between the two world wars, graphic arts, painting and sculpture in Cuba appeared to be ruled by the influence of the artistic vanguard of the twentieth century, reinforced by the firm contacts established with the centers of Art Deco: Paris and, later, New York. The arrival of the new visual arts concepts in Havana occurred via the graphic arts, thanks to cultural publications such as *Atuel* (1927–1928), *Revista de Avance* (1927–1930), the magazine *La Habana* (1930) and the magazine of the *Diario de la Marina* (1927–1930), especially after new ideas regarding illustrations and typography were introduced. As one can see from the preceding dates, these were short-lived publications. The work of the so-called "entertainment magazines" such as *Carteles*, but particularly *Social*, was more consistent and important. The contributions made by *Social* (1916–1933) are perhaps due to its relatively long life, the excellence of its text, and its cadre of well-qualified designers, headed by its director, Conrado Walter Massaguer (1889–1965).

Meanwhile, painting and sculpture were integrating similar principles, supported by the work of Cubans who had traveled to Paris to study. The works produced there sustained the emerging climate of rebirth that can be discerned in the 1920s. To resist the monotony imposed by rigorous academic teachings and adapt the lexicon of different media to modern life were the general criteria that resulted in an artistic practice derived from the progressive stylistic trends of the vanguard. The "draftsmen" (the title "graphic designer" was not yet in common usage) can be credited with sensitizing the artistic community to the new expressive modalities. Cuban artists would take on that chic version of Arte Moderno that in some ways represented Art Deco. In this fashion they contributed to the environment of renewal that was changing the very image of the city.

Jorge Mañach, first a painter and then a noted writer, underscored proof of this development in 1924 when he cited the work of an Arabic painter from Montparnasse, Radda, who exhibited surrealist tendencies. He extolled the painter's work, which appeared in the Asociación de Pintores y Escultores of the capital, for sounding the clarion for the new art. The call was immediately heeded by the "draftsmen" and progressive critics, who would use esthetic judgments to contribute to the expansion of the art form through the use of illustrations, humor and commercial propaganda or magazine covers. Graphic artists with forceful personalities, such as Jaime Valls (1883–1955) and José Hernández Cárdenas (1904–1957), were recognized at the time for embracing

Afro-Cuban themes, a significant development in such a racially and culturally mixed nation. When the Salón de Arte Moderno (1927) in the Asociación de Pintores y Escultores—organized by the "revista 1927" (the *Revista de Avance*)—was inaugurated, there was already a cultural milieu that this event could exploit, enrich, and elevate to a significant level. Even if this exhibit was timid in nature when compared to the European avant-garde, in Havana it carried an earth-shattering power. The inclusion of a painting by Antonio Gattorno, who had just arrived from Europe, was considered a focal point within the movement.

In the following years the "modern" tendency seems to have been projected onto the shared intuition that the urgency of these changes should involve a formulation resting on basic issues of Cuban art. It is well known that in the national context, sculpture lagged behind other areas in the visual arts. Once again, the importance of Cuban artists who studied in Paris must be underscored. One, Juan José Sicre, would become mentor to a generation that included such important artists as Ernesto Navarro, Rita Longa, Teodoro Ramos Blanco, and Florencio Gelabert, all of whom created significant studio work but whose major distinction is based on their contribution to monumental sculpture. The human figure attracted the interest of all of these artists and became the central theme of the sculpture found within the defining characteristics of Art Deco. It can be said that, given the quality and quantity of these works, there was a definite blossoming of this expressive style, and nothing created before or since can match it. The reliefs and the sheer volume and abundance of media (plaster, stone, cement, bronze) expressed the efforts of the sculptors and created an important chapter in the history of art in Cuba.

Facing page: José Hernández Cárdenas (Matanzas, 1904–La Habana, 1957), portrait of Pedro Valer, 1927, published in *Social* magazine.

GRAPHICS

The desire to imbue graphic arts with a new personality was transmitted largely via magazines, posters and announcements. Massaguer was its talented promoter. In addition to founding *Social*, he was the editor of other fine publications and he established the first photolithography plant in Latin America. Massaguer was an impressive caricaturist and illustrator—most definitely in the category of "draftsman"—and contributed to such American publications as the *New Yorker*, *Vanity Fair*, *American Magazine*, and the *New York American*. Although he was not the most important Art Deco illustrator of the moment, the considerable imprint of this style in his work reflects its typical ambience and personality. He designed many covers, and his watercolors and drawings, which appeared regularly, defined representative types of the era, such as the flapper and the *garçonne*. Also associated with *Social*, as its assistant artistic director, was Rafael Angel Surís, a painter and illustrator of considerable standing who was responsible for the inside pages of the publication until he moved to New York, where he worked for *Life* magazine and *Harper's Bazaar*. Cuban graphic arts gave rise to such artists as Jaime Valls, Enrique García Cabrera, José Manuel Acosta, Enrique Riverón, Rafael Lillo Botet, Carlos Fernández Méndez, Carlos Sánchez and Pedro Valer, to whom Hernández Cárdenas (yet another talented graphic artist) dedicated a full-page caricature in *Social*.

Carlos Fernández Méndez (born in 1901) is considered among the pioneers of modern graphic design. His assimilation of cutting-edge European ideas, defined by elegance and refinement, is exemplary, as is his unfailing sense for typography, essential to the transmission of ideas. He designed covers for *Social*, *Bohemia* and *Romances*; and posters and ads for companies such as Bourjois, a perfume manufacturer.

Enrique García Cabrera (1893–1949) is an exceptionally important figure. It is necessary to cite his name under several headings because of the frequency and diligence with which he pursued painting, illustration, caricatures and poster work. He was the author of cover pages, caricatures, advertisements and illustrations for important publications. One can highlight, for example, his use of the theme of velocity during his association with the magazine *El Automóvil*. The posters that accompanied health campaigns, and those that identified radio stations, were also important. He is credited with the well-known image, so defined by its mood and style, created early on for the tobacco manufacturer Baire. Here he included an aerial view of a portion of Havana's Malecón and El Morro. He created the Decorative Arts chair at the Academia de Bellas Artes de San Alejandro.

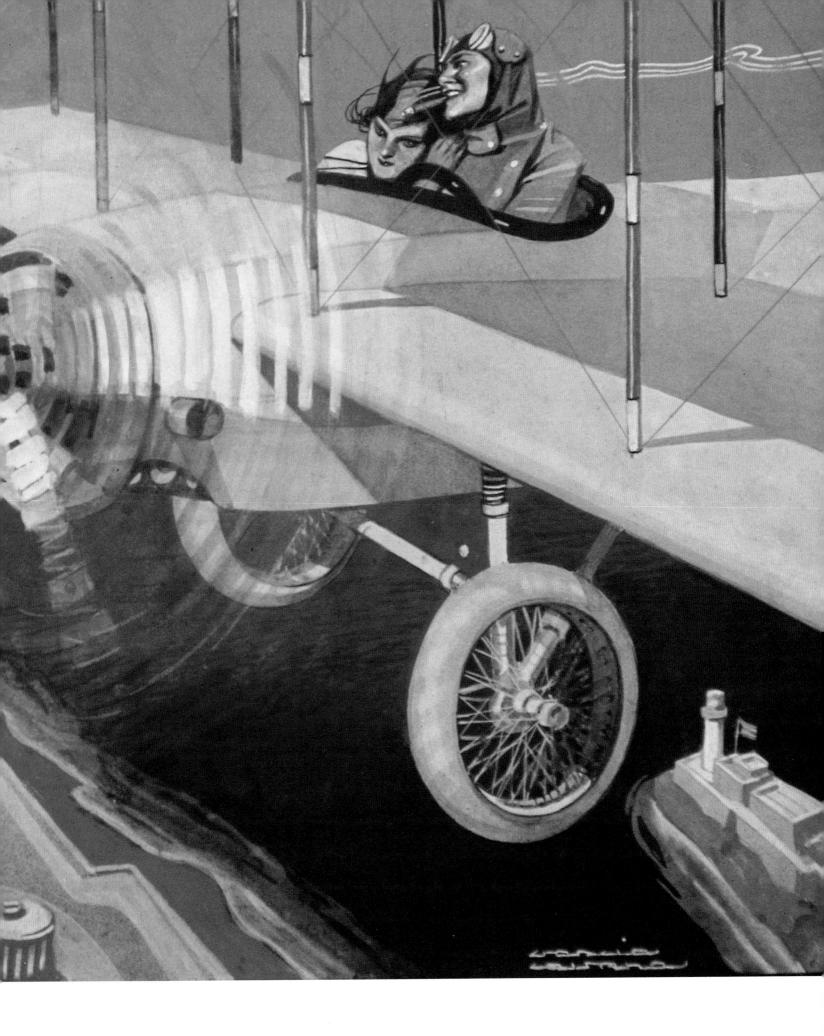

153

Facing page: cover page of *Social* by López Méndez.

Left: cover page of *Social* by Carlos Sánchez. Right: cover page of *Social* by Conrado Massaguer.

Left and right: advertisements designed by Jaime Valls.

Left: advertisement for cigars. Right: Rogelio Dalmau, fashion illustration for Casa Miranda appearing in *Social*, July 1930.

Jaime Valls (Tarragona, Spain, 1883–Havana, 1955), was one of the most active "modern" artists. He was a painter, draftsman, caricaturist, designer and solidly trained sculptor. He was a pioneer in the development of the Afro-Cuban theme in Cuba's modern art. Valls influenced advertising esthetically through his own work and as owner and director of an advertising agency. He had a great interest in themes associated with the Machine Age.

The work of Rogelio Dalmau (Havana, 1900–1954) is marked by his long professional career in Paris. The worlds of fashion and entertainment would occupy all of his attention, and it was to these fields that he primarily contributed. In spite of his success, and his distance from Cuba, his presence was affirmed there through his collaborations with illustrated Cuban magazines and through exhibits of sketches for fashion and furniture he had created in Europe.

SOCIAL

40c

MARZO 1927

C. W. MARQUER, DIRECTO

LA HABANA, CUBA

Enrique Riverón, who shared the tendency to incorporate progressive European artistic thought, traveled to Europe in 1924 on a grant after enjoying relative success in Cuba. There he collaborated with Madrid-based publications and became involved with a group of Cuban artists who resided in Montparnasse. In 1927 he exhibited his Parisian works that reflected Caribbean life in pure Deco style, as well as an earlier anthology he had produced for the soap manufacturer Jabón Candado, attributed to 1922. He developed a dynamic approach that included collaborations with Cuban, Chilean, and American magazines as well as animations for the Walt Disney movies *Sleeping Beauty* and *Ferdinand the Bull*. He finally settled in the United States, where he continued to develop both abstract and popular Afro-Cuban styles, as he had done since the thirties. The world of fashion produced a distinguished graphic artist, Rogelio Dalmau, who maintained links to Havana while residing in Paris. Two women, Lily del Barrio and Esperanza Durruthy, contributed to this healthy modernization, albeit from different standpoints. The first, who was a Hollywood fashion correspondent, worked as a costume designer for Paramount films. Durruthy's work appeared frequently and covered a diverse range: from covers for Cuban magazines and a gouache of Greta Garbo, to a "cloche hat for ladies who wish to copy the design."

Graphics at that time covered this extensive range—and more. Illustrations depicted a measure of the rigor and shape of the island's people. Similarly, thanks to photography—either by Cubans or by foreign artists—Cubans were updated on various aspects of human life: from "La Habana Vista de Aeroplano," a reportage with photos by José López y López (which in fact had been taken from the Hotel Sevilla Biltmore in Havana), to the image of the Cuban lightweight boxing champion Eligio Sardiñas (Kid Chocolate), who consented to pose for Hajdu in his photographic studio, Rembrandt, on the Paseo del Prado, as part of a campaign supporting nudism.

The fame of Eligio Sardiñas (Kid Chocolate) was the net product of his pugilistic skill and the power of the media at the time. Before reaching the age of twenty, he was a world champion in his division, had a million pesos in the bank, a "breathtaking" car, and received a hundred letters daily from adoring fans. Meanwhile, publications around the world accorded him as much press as they would a movie star.

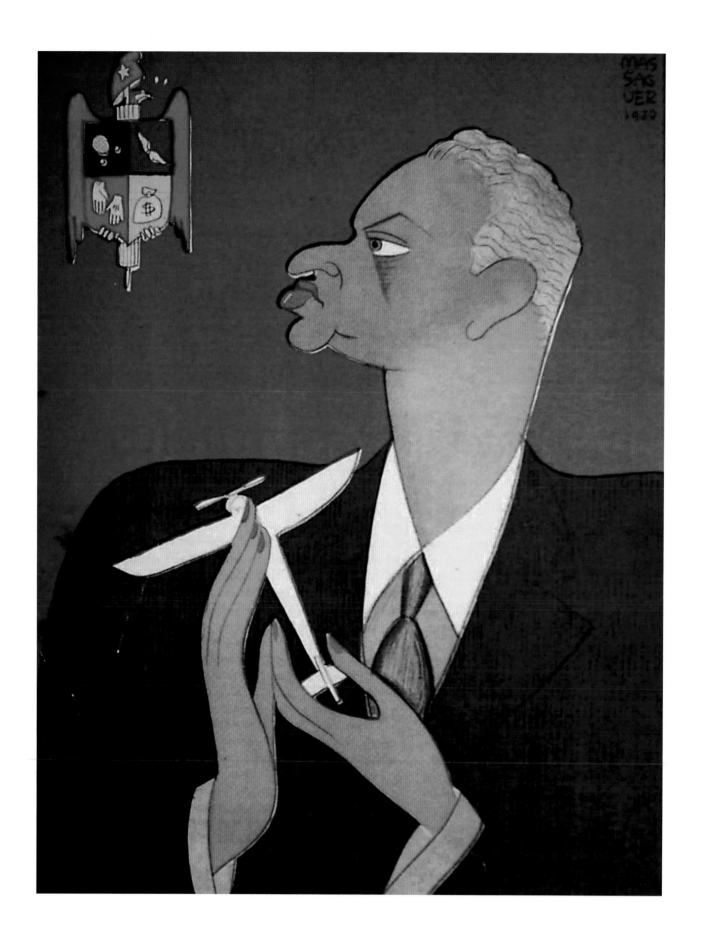

Massaguer in the excellent magazine *Social* and Andrés García (Andrés) in the magazine *Carteles* opened the way for illustrators with expressive styles at the high artistic level attained by Art Deco and were, at the same time, personally graced with a sense of fun and Cuban flavor. The barbed caricatures of Massaguer frequently attained the status of classics. This was achieved through his consummate talent in bringing out the close resemblance to the caricatured personality. Also worthy of consideration was his skill in reflecting social phenomena, as well as his sharp treatment of the zeal to be in fashion, or of the poseur: in short, the graphic commentary on that which prevailed in the environment and which was almost impossible to avoid elaborating upon in order to communicate in a fresh and masterful way with the public that bought the magazine.

Andrés, whose dedication went beyond the graphic by way of designs for theatrical production or artistic creation, found a kind of forum for himself on the covers of *Carteles*. He was able to express himself with technical command and a strong sense of genre that made them immediately recognizable. He managed, in exemplary creative production, to assimilate the most sophisticated vocabulary of the moment into an expression that supported his effectiveness in the most direct popular sense.

Like Massaguer, Surís became one of those graphic designers who succeeded in crossing the national frontier. He was active in the United States at publications like *Harper's Bazaar*, where he achieved a distinguished position thanks to the exceptional conditions at the time in the fashion world. Although he resided in America, he never lost contact with *Social*, a magazine that was comparable to the best there. Enrique García Cabrera had many occupations, among them artistic director of the department store Fin de Siglo and creator of ads for the best national publications.

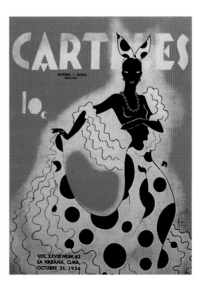

Facing page: Harry Guggenheim, ambassador of the United States of America, in Cuba, 1930, by Massaguer.

Right: Cover of *Carteles* magazine by Andrés.

Upper right: Fashion illustration by Surís.

Bottom right: Advertisement by García Cabrera.

PAINTING

It is difficult to characterize painting of this period within a Deco context, given the differences among the artists. Nonetheless, it is important to note that they are linked by a decorative perspective. This is not in any way a pejorative evaluation. Rather, it unites Cubans of this movement who evolved artistically through academic training in Cuba, travel to Europe—with Paris as their Mecca—and who were thus exposed to diverse currents of twentieth-century artistic thought. To underscore these concepts one can refer to the painter

Antonio Gattorno (La Habana, 1904–New York, 1981), *Mujeres en el Río*, 1927, oil on canvas, 193 x 117 cm.

Amelia Peláez (1896–1968) and one of her exceptional works, namely her illustrations (1936) for the poem "La Agonía de Petronio" written by her uncle Julián del Casal. A reproduction of one of these appears in the introduction to this chapter. The influence of her professor, the Russian futurist Alexandra Exter, is clearly evident in Peláez's illustrations, as are those elements that Henri

Jorge Arche (Santo Domingo, Cuba 1905–Cádiz, Spain, 1956). Although his academic schooling was erratic, it nonetheless provided the technical skills essential to his profession as a painter. He graduated from the Academia de Bellas Artes de San Alejandro. His training as a "modern" artist, integral to the first generation of these painters in Cuba, is due to his direct, if unconventional, contact with artists who had taken the opportunity to live in Paris. One such teacher was Victor Manuel García, considered among the pioneers of the movement. In this way Arche was able to progress a great deal and create portraits appreciated for their clarity of line and round volumes. The hedonistic conception of his paintings, a complacent attitude toward his models, and the delightful manifestation of a pleasant atmosphere are equally important characteristics of his work. All of these aspects place him in the category of artists for whom narcissism was not a defect; on the contrary, it was their proper and fundamental raison d'être. The Retrato de la êscultora Rita Longa painted by Arche shows many of the artist's distinctive traits: an honest rendering of the model's personal characteristics, the deliberate elongation of the figure, the richness of the details and, in general, the penetrating analytical sense found in his best creations.

Canvas mural for the Hospital de Maternidad Obrera in Marianao by Enrique García Cabrera.

Matisse stated were an example of the "much sought integration between painting of the highest order and Art Deco." These traits include Peláez's taste for arabesques, the vivacity of color planes and yet again a profound decorative sensibility. Knowing that the Cuban painter was a longtime admirer of Matisse assists us in understanding her art.

Antonio Gattorno (La Habana, 1904–New York, 1980) was, like Amelia Peláez, a distinguished member of the first generation of "modern" Cuban painters. He, like other artists, graduated from the Academia de Bellas Artes San Alejandro, and began his studies in Europe in 1921 thanks to a study grant.

First he traveled to Italy, then to Spain, later to Belgium and finally to France, where he spent his last three European years. He returned in 1926, and the following year—a time noted for its importance to modern art in Cuba— exhibited his works, a summary of his European experiences including some of the paintings he completed there. Among the latter is *Mujeres en el Río*, a Deco representation of an idyllic tropical scene based on monumental female nudes, which appears to echo the reflections of the Polish-Russian painter Tamara Lempicka: "...a painting must be sharp and clean." This holds especially true for both artists (who shared an admiration of Ingres's artistic precision) in this era ruled by machines. The still-life found in the lower-right corner of the cited work seems to pay homage to Cézanne, and, in general, the tone of this piece certainly transmits the notion that the lessons of the Paris school were well learned. Gattorno, respected by the most distinguished intellectuals of his era, later changed his approach to creative art. His classification as an Art Deco painter up to and including this time, however, remains true. Jaime Valls was a distinguished painter as well as an influential graphic artist.

In 1928 the Cuban historian Emilio Roig de Leuchsenring recognized Gattorno and his contemporary Víctor Manuel García as epitomizing "the admirable and valuable, although isolated, efforts of creating an art native to the Americas." After viewing the twenty paintings Valls had produced for a showing, Leuchsenring recognized Valls's absolute commitment to Cuban art. He referred to the artist's groundbreaking vision of the Afro-Cuban figure, within the perspective of "modernist" characteristics. When discussing Art Deco, the emphasis is on those artists who were distinct from each other and who manifested these characteristics with varying intensity and frequency. When these artists introduced the new principles of the European vanguard in Cuba, they followed different routes: Victor Manuel García, the leading artist of the first generation of "modern" painters, reflected his awe of the bucolic Postimpressionism of Paul Gauguin, who was radically opposed to the assimilation of Italian Futurism as exemplified by Marcelo Pogolotti. These artists and their differences exemplify the work of the admirers of Arte Nuevo in Cuba. Jorge

Mario Carreño, *Nacimiento de las Antillas*, 1940, oil on canvas, 69 x 86.5 cm.

Mario Carreño (Havana, 1913–Santiago de Chile, 1999) was part of what is considered the second generation of "modern" Cuban painters. A precocious, anxious and cosmopolitan artist, he sought his teachers informally through a series of trips abroad. In this way he mingled with such notable figures as the Dominican Jaime Colson and the Mexican David Alfaro Siqueiros. His work is distinguished by his design, his use of sketches and a conscious awareness with regard to the artistic avant-garde (marked by the substitution of the *C* in his surname with a *K*). He then cultivated a style tinged by social awareness and the decorativeness of Art Deco, so suitable in the advertising media within which it developed. Deco elements are also present in *Nacimiento de las Antillas*, 1940. Here there is a clear allusion to late works of Giorgio de Chirico. It represents the type of art in which the attractive treatment of the topic creates unlimited esthetic enjoyment.

Arche and Mario Carreño, two outstanding painters who belonged to two successive generations of Cuban artists, also freely used Deco stylistic forms—and they were not alone. In Cuba, Art Deco painting aspired to creatively challenge the artistic influences being launched from foreign lands. These were translated into a language that adopted its own vibrations and the rhythm of the vernacular, according to the requirements of the task at hand, while maintaining the style's grace and cadence.

Oil paintings such as *La Rumbera*, 1926, won Jaime Valls (1883–1955) special recognition in the press as a result of his development of Afro-Cuban themes.

SCULPTURE

Cuban sculpture of the period reached a level of development that allows this to be considered a Golden Age. The master of "modern" Cuban sculpture, Juan José Sicre (1898–1974) , a follower of Bourdelle, is considered Cuba's first great sculptor. After his return from Paris in 1926, he received several important commissions. The October–December 1932 issue of the magazine *Arquitectura y Artes Decorativas* mentioned that the artist had created bas-reliefs for one of the first Havana homes in the Art Deco style, that of the Francisco Argüelles family, as well as for the residence of Ramón Crusellas, a soap manufacturer. The art critic writes that "decorative" sculpture was incorporated with the architecture. A decade later the Cuban critic Guy Pérez Cisneros agreed, writing that the sculptor's work was "somewhat stylized and therefore decorative." Included in his extensive oeuvre is his contribution to the group that comprises the Mausoleo de los Veteranos de las Guerras de Independencia de Cuba, and the seated figure of José Martí for the Memorial de la Plaza Cívica. Following the official announcement of the contest for Martí's monument in 1938, the project underwent several planning stages. Finally, Sicre's design was selected the winner: a classic temple with his sculpture at its center. However, the stepped tower designed by the architects Labatut-Otero-Varela and the seated Martí, made of Cuban marble, were not completed until 1958. Among the successful "decorative" sculptors was Ernesto Navarro (Havana, 1904–1975). In 1928 "three significant works" by the artist were shown in the Salón de Humoristas y Artes, three busts of Lina, Minerva and Androgynous placed within a "modern" esthetic, a far cry from the audacity found in *Maternidad*, carved in wood and found in the Museo Nacional de Bellas Artes. Other distinguished works carved in stone include those for the Plaza Finlay in Marianao and the Palacio de Convenciones y Deportes in El Vedado (no longer in existence). *Fuente* (1942) may still be admired in the Parque de los Mártires, near the Paseo del Prado. Rita Longa (Havana, 1912–2000) was a sculptor who left a bounty of monumental works in the Deco style. She was the most influential and distinguished figure among the excellent artists of the movement. Teodoro Ramos Blanco (Havana, 1902–1972) and Florencio Gelabert (Havana, 1904–1995) are also included in this group of artists. *Madre e Hijo* (1939), sculpted by Ramos Blanco, crowns the façade of the Clínica de Maternidad Obrera of Marianao. The work expressed a theme represented in other works of his, including one version, dated 1934, for the Hospital de Maternidad América Arias in El Vedado, and another in 1950 for a hospital complex in Old Havana. His expansion of the Afro-Cuban theme, and his expertise in tech-

Rita Longa (Havana, 1912–2000) was a student of Sicre for two years at the Academia de Bellas Artes de San Alejandro, until she left her studies. Her initial work in plaster shows, early on, her enthusiasm for the possibilities of "decorative" sculpture. Her work demonstrates the fluidity and rhythms, as well as the elegance, characteristic of Art Deco in general. She quickly addressed the mastery of open public spaces and succeeded in designing a project for the Fuente de los Mártires, located in the city's historic center. The project dates from 1941. The model for the fountain—whose hull was designed by Honorato Colette—and the plaster cast were made the following year. However, the work was interrupted and not concluded until 1947.

niques such as direct carving, accent the importance of his work. *Friso*, by Gelabert, received a bronze medal in the XXII Salón de Bellas Artes (1940). A later version of this work, used as a decorative panel, appeared in the building of the Calle Habana 563. About 1945 he created *El Ara de la Patria*, a bronze relief

The trilogy of monumental works for which Rita Longa has garnered fame is comprised of the *Fuente de los Mártires* (1941–1947), *Grupo Familiar* (1947), a family of deer cast in bronze and placed at the entrance of the Zoological Park of Nuevo Vedado, and the *Virgen del Camino*, which gave its name to the park where it was erected. The artist's discourse appears centered on the figure of the female as its principal inspirational motif, which she continued to develop using Deco stylistic rules through the 1950s. In the early fifties the popular sculptress created *Ballerina*, a work placed at the entrance of the Tropicana Cabaret and which became a symbol of this well-known nightspot. She also created the bronze *Illusion* and the relief *Musas* that decorate the Teatro Payret of Paseo del Prado, as well as the marble *Piedad*, the crowning expression of her religious convictions, which graces the simple vault of the Aguilera family in the Cementerio Cristóbal Colón. Within this roster is also *Santa Rita de Cascia* (1943), a work in plaster that was never cast in bronze, conceived for the main altar of the church of the same name. This statue was relegated, at a much later date, to a side chapel, "since this type of modern image did not awaken the devotion of the faithful." She is our Deco sculptor par excellence and its most prolific, dedicated advocate.

at the center of the Mausoleo de los Veteranos de las Guerras de Independencia de Cuba. This commission was important in the work of a man who, in addition, was dedicated to the exploration of materials such as concrete, an ideal medium for the sculptures "applied" to buildings. If, as we believe, every city has feelings and the capacity to experience pride in those who gave it a soul, then Havana should be proud of its Art Deco sculpture.

Among the many works of an urban environmental character that were built in public places like Havana City during the Deco era, four can be singled out that follow diverse expressions within one stylistic line. Depicting the native human couple provided the opportunity for Ernesto Navarro to create in 1941 a fountain—which he never completed in the space allocated—within the Plaza de los Mártires project. *Madre e Hijo* (1950), by Teodoro Ramos Blanco, places a tender accent beside the stairway of a maternity and children's hospital in Old Havana. This is his third version of the subject—this time in marble. The previous examples—one in stone, the other in majolica—were also de-

signed for hospitals. Later, in 1952, Arnold Serrú redesigned a kind of obelisk which on its two sides combined bronze high reliefs with stones from the seashore to commemorate the death of Cuban sailors in World War II. No human element was chosen at the time of creating the black marble pillar, which was erected in 1931—dedicated to the memory of the members of the Chinese quarter of Cuba who fought in the Ten Years' War of liberation from Spain.

Facing page: Juan José Sicre (1898–1974), seated figure of José Martí (1938–1958), marble, José Martí Memorial.

Right: Juan José Sicre (1898–1974), *Fuente de las Antillas* (ca.1941), marble.

Below: Florencio Gelabert (1904–1995), detail of *Friso* (ca. 1939), cement.

BIBLIOGRAPHY

BOOKS

Alonso, Alejandro G. *Novecento Cubano*. Milano: Cronodata, 1995.

———. *La Obra Escultórica de Rita Longa*. La Habana: Letras Cubanas, 1998.

Álvarez Tabío, Enma. *Vida, Mansión y Muerte de la Burguesía Cubana*. La Habana: Letras Cubanas, 1989.

Arwas, Víctor. *Art Deco*. London, Academy Editions, 1982.

Bouillon, Jean-Paul. *Journal de L'Art Déco*. Genève: Skira, 1988.

Capitman Baer, Barbara. *Deco Delights*. New York: E. P. Dutton, 1988.

Carley, Rachel. *Cuba: 400 Years of Architectural Heritage*. New York: Whitney Library of Design, 1997.

Cerwinske, Laura. *Tropical Deco: The Architecture and Design of Old Miami Beach*. New York: Rizzoli, 1988.

Claridge, Laura. *Tamara Lempicka: A Life of Deco and Decadence*. London: Bloomsbury, 2000.

Cuevas, Juan de las. *500 Años de Construcciones en Cuba*. La Habana, Chavín, 2001.

Hillier, Bevis, and Stephen Scritt. *Art Deco Style*. London: Phaidon, 2003.

Morales, Juan Luis, Xavier Galmiche, and Giovanni Zanzi. *Havana: Districts of Light*. Paris: Vilo, 2001.

Rodríguez, Eduardo Luis. *La Habana: Arquitectura del Siglo XX*. Barcelona: Blume, 1998.

Sambricio, Carlos and Roberto Segre. *Arquitectura de la Ciudad de La Habana: Primera Modernidad*. Milan: Electa, 2000.

Sternau, Susan. *Art Deco: Flights of Artistic Fancy*. New York: Todtri, 1997.

Weber, Eva. *American Art Deco*. New York: Crescent Books, 1992.

———. *Art Deco*. New York: Gallery Books, 1989.

Weiss, Joaquín E. *Arquitectura Cubana Contemporánea*. La Habana: Cultural S.A., 1947.

———. *Medio Siglo de Arquitectura Cubana*. La Habana: Facultad de Arquitectura, Universidad de La Habana, 1951.

PERIODICALS

Cuban Reviews in the Deco Period
Álbum de Cuba

Anuario Cultural de Cuba

Arquitectura

Arquitectura y Artes Decorativas

Arte y Decoración

Cuba: Arquitectura y Artes Similares

El Arquitecto

Revista de Avance

Revista del Colegio de Arquitectos de La Habana

Social

PUBLICATIONS SUBSEQUENT TO THE DECO PERIOD

Journal of Decorative and Propaganda Arts 22 (1996), Cuba Theme Issue.

Segre, Roberto, Pilar Fernández, and Luz Merino. "El Art Deco en La Habana."
Temas 9, (1986): 56–59.

ACKNOWLEDGMENTS

A special thanks to Dr. Eusebio Leal Spengler, historian of the City of Havana, for his support.

Oficina del Historiador de la Ciudad

Museo Nacional de Bellas Artes

Casa de las Américas

Biblioteca del Centro Nacional de Conservación, Restauración y Museología

Centro Cultural Teatro América

Familia Menéndez-Sigarroa

Doctor Carlos Amat

Ana María Alvarez Tabío

Avelina Alcalde

Alicia Pérez Malo

Arquitecto José A. Choy

Adriano Moretti

Painter Luis Rodríguez Noa and his wife Elaine

Staff of the National Museum of Contemporary Cuban Ceramics, Havana

Vecinos del Edificio López Serrano

Special thanks to David Unger for his major contribution to this edition of the book.

INDEX